THE PROMISE
Between Us

∽ NOVELLA THREE ∾

NAOMI FINLEY

ISBN: 978-1-989165-12-6

Cover designer: Victoria Cooper Art
Website: www.facebook.com/VictoriaCooperArt

Editor: Scripta Word Services
Website: scripta-word-services.com

READING ORDER FOR SERIES

Novels:
A Slave of the Shadows: Book One
A Guardian of Slaves: Book Two
A Whisper of War: Book Three (Coming Soon)

Novellas:
The Black Knight's Tune: Novella One
The Master of Ships: Novella Two
The Promise Between Us: Novella Three
The Fair Magnolia: Novella Four

Novels can be read alone or with the novella series.
The author's shorter works are best read in the suggested
order.

Prologue

Charleston, South Carolina, 1832

I CLUTCHED MY BABE TO MY BREAST, CURLING TIGHTER against the wall of the pen, yearning to fade from the slave traders who'd soon come to retrieve us. Within iron-railed cages, I waited with forty-three other slaves rounded up from plantations along our journey to Charleston. The excited voices of planters and purchasers conversing in the open-air auction echoed off the stone corridor walls.

Terror of the outcome of the day glistened on brows and shone brightly in the eyes of the men and women crammed into the small holding cells. Spent tears stained the cheeks of children old enough to understand what was about to happen, and they clung to their mammies and pappies. Those too young to comprehend used stones to draw in the dirt floor while others had fallen into a peaceful sleep in their parents' laps.

I glanced down at Mary Grace, who slept heavily. Breath lightly whistled through her lips, and a soft smile played on her cheeks. Tracing a finger over her sweat-soaked hair, then her perfect mouth, I wanted nothing more than to return the babe to the protection of my womb.

Tears I'd expelled from Masa Adams's plantation to Charleston left my eyes scratchy and red. I wept for what lay ahead and for the love I'd left behind—my African prince. The man who'd loved Mary Grace as his own, and had taught me to love again. I needed him to wrap me in his big, strong arms and whisper words of encouragement to ease the anxiety gurgling like a creek within me.

Early in the morning, the slave traders had come to the pens and ordered we strip before dousing us with buckets of cold water. Our bodies were scrubbed raw, but with care not to break the skin. Then we were greased to infer health and youthfulness, and those with scars that might reveal a troublesome slave were painted with tar to deceive the purchasers. Women's hair was braided or covered with a head rag before they and the children were clothed in clean Negro cloth shifts. Men were given matching trousers and shirts.

Next to me, a man adjusted his position against the wall and bumped my arm. He mumbled an apology. Our gazes met, and the gutted pain in his dark eyes reflected the terrors that had thrashed his body the night before and caused him to cry out, then sit upright to stare endlessly at the wall across the pen.

He looked at Mary Grace, his jaw tight and flexing. "She your only one?"

"Yes, and de last, ef I can help et. My heart can't handle no more loss."

"Death be easier den having another," he said before

resting his head against the cool of the stone wall and closing his eyes. I stared at him a moment longer, wondering what fate had marked his soul with such hardness.

The sound of shoes scuffing on stone pulled us all to our feet. My heart hammered against my ribcage as paralyzing fear gripped me. It was time. Now our future would be assigned for us, as the white men once again played God with our lives. "Please, Lard, don't let dem take my babe," I whispered silently.

Two men came to stand in front of us and I crept back, trying to disappear into the others. My knees trembled, and sweat poured down my inner thighs, trickling over my bare feet. I slumped into the man behind me, and firm hands reached out to steady me.

"I know you skeered, but you got to be strong for de chile 'til you got no other choice." His whisper was gruff yet comforting.

A tear slid down my cheek. *How?* I screamed inside. Life without my daughter was a life I couldn't survive. Before, I'd thought that without my family I couldn't go on. Then, when they ripped Big John from me I crumbled, and only Mary Grace's wiggling body had pushed me forward and helped me stay upright as I was put in a wagon. Big John had run alongside the wagon until he reached the property line, where he had to stop or be shot down like an old dog. Brushing at the tears marring my vision, I'd seared every last detail of him into my memory.

When we passed by the swampland surrounding Charleston, alligators' heads broke the surface of the murky waters, their beady eyes patrolling with anticipation.

I envisioned leaping over the side of the wagon and wading out into the waters and letting the creatures maul my body until nothing remained but my bones, bare of my human flesh. Then the cooing of the babe in my arms and her small fist striking my chest had ceased the crazed thoughts, and I curled in the corner of the wagon to feed her as the slave trader positioned on the seat beside the driver watched on.

The iron gate rattled as keys were thrust into the lock. The auctioneer entered with another man I recalled from the previous day. They moved throughout the pen, inspecting us all.

The auctioneer stopped in front of me. "You're a pretty thing. You should fetch a hefty profit." Prying my mouth open, he inspected my teeth before circling me. His hand gripped a handful of my buttocks, and I froze. My breath caught. He grunted and inhaled deeply before he released his hold, circled again, and squeezed my breast before moving down to the tender place between my legs. I cringed at his touch but stood still, enduring the inspection.

"Yes, a fine profit." His blue eyes gleamed with satisfaction.

I hadn't realized my grip on Mary Grace until she began to fuss. Easing my hold, I swayed her gently in my arms. The auctioneer said to the other man, "I'm wondering if we might sell her alone without the child. Market her as untouched. Mr. Thames likes them like that. What do you say, Lewis?"

No! Again, I looked upon a white man's face. Tears

bit at the corners of my eyes. *Lard, please! I'll die.* Noting my fear he postured, thrusting out his chest. I dropped my gaze to stare at his boots. I prayed for the cruelest death to befall him, a disease that would cause the flesh to peel from his bones.

"Ain't no way you can sell dat one lak she be pure," said a deep voice behind me. I eyed the man chained to me as he continued. "She let me have my way wid her last night, and you won't be fooling no one 'bout de looseness dat heats between her legs."

My flesh burned with humiliation, but my heart swelled with gratitude at the man's attempt to keep them from separating me from my daughter.

The auction masa struck the wall by the man's head with the butt of his whip. "Silence, you dog! Breathe another word and there won't be anything left of your hide to sell."

"I could save you de trouble," the man said, as though he had a death wish.

The auction masa's hand clenched at his side at the rebellion of the man, but to harm him now meant he would forgo the profit an attractive, strong man like him would bring.

"All right, line them up. The good people of Charleston await."

Herding us into a single line, they pushed us forward, down the corridor toward the auction block. The clanging of the chains secured around our ankles sang loud and haunting against the stone ground. Soon the human train halted, and our ankle shackles were removed. Traders sectioned the men off from the women and children. The first man took his station on the platform, and the auctioneer's voice penetrated the afternoon, and the shouts of purchasers rose to meet his. Minutes ticked past and the man's future was decided.

"Sold!" the auctioneer called.

The slave twisted to look in my direction, his dark eyes dripping with fear as the piercing wail from a woman split the chatter of the auction. Turning, I saw the woman drop to her knees, rocking back and forth, her hands extended to the heavens.

A guard charged at her and yanked her to her feet, shaking her roughly. "Shut your mouth if you know what's good for you."

The woman's sobs muffled to a soft whimper.

I glanced back at the slave man as they led him toward us. His shoulders shook with silent sobs. He reached for his woman, but the slave trader elbowed him on. The pain of their separation stirred the ache of my longing for the gentle giant who visited my daydreams. The white men could take my body, but they would never take my mind or the memories of the man that owned my heart. "Ain't no white men's auction dat could sell dat," I whispered through gritted teeth.

My cellmates' fates were determined, one after another. Women, men, and children openly grieved as their families were torn apart. The guards stepped in to silence them and quell unease amongst the whites.

The man who'd come to Mary Grace's and my rescue mounted the steps and moved to the middle of the platform. His shoulders sloped forward and his head hung, the fight he had shown earlier a fleeting memory.

Using the butt of his whip, the auctioneer hoisted the man's head. "We got a prize picking today, folks. This buck is a skilled blacksmith. And one of the finest you will find." He started rambling off prices, and the bidding began.

"Sold," the auctioneer said moments later.

Again, the man was escorted past us to await his new master to settle his debt and come to retrieve him. As the man shuffled by, I grabbed his wrist. "May de Lard watch over you," I said.

He stopped, his dark, hollow eyes chiseling through mine. "Ain't no God in dis place."

"Come on, move." The guard prodded him onward.

The blacksmith moved down the line as instructed. A woman reached out and touched his shoulder. "Keep heart, James."

The blacksmith grunted and continued down the aisle of slaves.

"Surviving is how we win." A man held out shackled wrists, beseeching us all. "Dey may divide our families, but dey can't take our souls."

The blacksmith paused in front of the man. "You be a man widout a family, 'cause you know not what you speak."

"Friend, what have you lost?"

"Evvything," he said, followed by a gasp as a blow to the back of the head from the guard pushed him on.

A calloused hand grabbed my arm. "Move along. It's your turn."

With weighted legs, I climbed the steps and allowed a man to move me into position.

"This handsome Negress is a domestic slave and will make some family a good nursemaid." The auctioneer's words muffled as I stood rigid, looking out over the crowd of eager faces studying me as one would when purchasing a racehorse.

My gaze fell on a woman swollen with child. Something in the way she looked at me puckered my brow. Kindness bestowed on us coloreds by the whites was a rarity. But the woman's face reflected concern as she looked from me to my child. She leaned close to the man who stood tall and proud beside her, a handsome man with blond hair and a firm jaw. He tilted his ear to hear the woman, and his eyes fell on me. My heart stuck in my throat. They exchanged a few words; he patted her hand resting on his arm and nodded.

"We start the bidding on the Negress," the auctioneer said, and I realized he made no mention of my child. *No!* My gaze swung back to the pregnant woman to find her eyes locked on me.

Find mussy! I sent her a silent plea, willing her to hear me. One mother to another. *Please help me.* I held Mary Grace tighter to my chest.

"Sold!" came again from the auctioneer and panic surged within me. "Number Thirteen goes to Mr. Hendricks."

The crowd became a blur, and panic seized me as a trader stepped forward and tried to pry Mary Grace from my arms. "No!" I said, my voice cracked and hoarse. "You can't take my chile." I crept back, swatting at the man's hands.

"Cause a scene, and I'll see to it your child doesn't live to see the dawn," the auctioneer whispered in my ear, his fingers biting into the flesh of my upper arm.

Fear drummed in my chest.

A woman's uneasy voice lifted above the crowd. "We wish to purchase the mother and the child."

The auctioneer twisted to seek the speaker of the claim and his hold loosened on my arm. Looking askance, I saw the pregnant woman had pushed her way through the crowd to stand below the platform.

The blond gentleman also pushed through the crowd, a look of bewilderment etched across his face. "Olivia!" He tugged on her arm.

The auctioneer laughed. "Mr. Hendricks, is your wife making the financial decisions for your household now?"

"Watch it, Thompson." A firm warning flared in the husband's eyes. "As my wife said, we wish to purchase mother and child."

"Have it your way, then. You can settle your debt after the auction."

The husband guided his wife away from the crowd, and as I was led off the block I saw them immersed in conversation. Most men wouldn't abide a public display of sass from a woman, and I feared the punishment she would receive from her husband for coming to my aid. She had forgotten her place, but in doing so she saved me from being separated from my daughter and, for that, I'd serve her well for all the days I belonged to her.

In the pen I sat waiting with the others sold, feeding Mary Grace, when the soft scent of jasmine touched my nose. Looking up, I found the dark-haired woman from the auction standing at the bars watching me.

"What is the baby's name?" she asked.

I removed the baby from my breast and covered myself. Rising to my feet, I placed the sleeping baby over my shoulder and gently patted her back. "Mary Grace," I said.

"Is she a good baby?"

"Mostly."

"That's good." A soft smile touched her brilliant green eyes. "This is my first child." She caressed her stomach affectionately. "As my time draws near, I wish my mother were alive to help me. I'm afraid I don't know the first thing about raising a child."

I crept closer to the bars. "Dey mostly need feeding and changing and a li'l bit of love."

She laughed—a pretty, musical sound. "You make it sound so simple. Yet I fear I'll have one of those babies that scream for hours upon end." Her merriment slipped and worry played on her face.

"I'll help you," I said, finding myself wanting to ease her anxiety. I recalled the day when I'd found out I was with child, and the fear that plagued me, as it did most slaves. Little pleasure came from the birth of a child to a slave, because family became leverage the whites used against us. If we didn't follow what the masas said, the ones we loved most would be taken, often never to be seen again.

Missus's eyes held mine, her expression sincere. "I'd like that more than you know."

"Olivia, there you are." The husband appeared. "I told you to wait by the wagon."

"I know. But I wanted to make an acquaintance with our child's nursemaid."

A look of helpless appeal glinted in his eyes. "Surely you could've waited 'til we were on our way home." He glanced at me, and I inched back under his unnerving stare.

Would he want from me what Masa Adams had desired? I shivered, choking back my fear. But when my new masa turned his attention back to his wife, I noted the tenderness softening the tautness in his face, and I hoped the lovely, dark-haired creature on the other side of the bars was enough to satisfy his needs.

"You're impossible," he said with a shake of his head.

His wife bestowed on him a soft smile and stroked his arm, showing visible affection, a gesture between husband and wife that society scowled upon. I'd once heard of whites placing a board in the marriage bed to separate the man and woman, yet white babes kept coming, and any slave with something between their ears grasped the plank was as ridiculous as the inventor of such an idea.

Masa's eyes paused on the missus's lips, and I knew the plank got put by the bedside often enough. He looked away at the sound of the cell guard unlocking the gate.

"You." He pointed at me. "Come on."

❧ CHAPTER ❧
One

Livingston Plantation, Three Years Later

ISSUS OLIVIA WAS MISSING. NIGHT FADED AND THE morning sun guttered through the live oaks and soon dissolved into the afternoon, spreading unrest throughout the plantation. I eyed the lane from the front veranda, hoping to catch a glimpse of Masa Charles and Missus Olivia. My tension peaked with each drawn-out, lamenting tune of the mourning dove perched on the limb of a nearby magnolia tree.

Last night I cradled and sang to the little miss until her tears turned into hiccups and exhaustion overcame her. Swelling had swallowed my ankles from a night of treading the hallways and veranda into the early hours of the morning.

With no sign of the masas doom rested on my shoulders, and the chill of the unknown snaked up and down my arms. Something was amiss. I felt it in my bones.

Masa Charles had ridden off in a panic when the missus didn't return the first evening. He took Miller, the overseer, and some of the other menfolk with him, but they returned after dark without the masa. I'd slipped out the back door to listen in on the men as they watered their horses at the trough.

"Dark as hell out there. He won't be able to see a damn thing." Miller had snorted, removing his hat and slapping it against his leg to lift the dust. "That woman's going to get him killed. I say it's about time Mr. Hendricks took her in hand. A good beating would do her some good. Always going around sticking her pretty nose in men's affairs, and taking off when she sees fit. His weakness when it comes to his wife ain't much different than her daddy's. The woman has an eerie hold over men. If it were my wife, I'd let the gators have her and nab myself another. Ain't got no time for a disobedient woman, no more than I do a darkie."

Then he had turned and spotted me. His lewd gaze lingered and I pulled my shawl snuggly around me, trying to hide my body from him. Instinct told me to run inside because, without the missus home to protect me, Miller might get it into his numb skull to act upon the lust shadowing his icy blue eyes. He'd been eyeing me since the day I'd come to Livingston, but thanks to my position as a domestic slave—caregiver to the little miss and the missus—I'd avoided his snare.

The need for news on the missus quelled my desire to retreat into the refuge of the big house. See, I'd done what slaves warned themselves against: you don't grow feelings for the ones entrusted to your care. I had never let myself care for no white person before, and to love one was laughable—I'd considered them downright unlovable, in fact. But it had happened nonetheless, and I'd come to love the little miss and missus like kin. Before I grasped it, they had snuck their way into the soft place inside me I reserved for Big John and Mary Grace.

This afternoon the sun beamed high and bright over the fields speckled with folks working the ground. I paced the front veranda. My cuticles bled and burned from my constant gnawing.

What if something unspeakable had happened to Missus Olivia? The low country animals could have carried her body off somewhere. Or maybe…someone had kidnapped her? And were holding her for ransom? Relentless, tormenting possibilities played in my mind.

"Rita gal, you got to stop tearing up de floorboards." Ketty, the plantation's cook and my dearest friend, clambered up the front steps. "You ain't doing anyone a lick o' good, out here wid your eyes pinned to dat dere lane." She straightened her reedy frame, rubbing an ache in her lower back.

"I worried sick 'bout Missus Olivia. Somepin' ain't right. She always comes back."

"I knowed et." New channels seemed to have mapped her weathered face overnight. "I worried too. But some folkses are more concerned 'bout what's gwine to happen ef Masa doesn't return." She nudged her head at Miller, who sat upon his horse, making his rounds in the fields. I'd seen an image like him in Missus Olivia's books. I believe the whites called him "Napoleon." He sat upon his horse with his fist resting on his thigh and his sharp chin arched up. I could almost taste the overpowering odor of onions that roiled my stomach whenever the man was near.

I spat over the rail of the veranda into Missus's roses,

which lay sleeping with the approach of winter. "Dey got good cause to worry. Dat man got no care for de missus or us. Acting lak he all high and mighty up on dat horse of his, when he ain't any smarter dan de nigras he lak to call stupid. Can't read. Can't write. Jus' lak de rest o' us. But only a fool be forgitting he got all de power widout de masa and missus 'round." Anxiety at the thought of what a man like Miller was capable of spread like lice in the quarters, jumping from Ketty's head to mine.

Ketty wiped the palms of her chapped hands on her apron, her gaze flitting down the lane. Purchased by Missus Olivia's pappy, Masa Shaw, she'd been a slave at Livingston from the beginning. Ol' Missus Shaw was too frail, and her milk had never come in, so Ketty had been bought as a wet nurse for Missus Olivia. Broke poor Ketty and the missus's heart when Masa Shaw took to thinking the missus was caring for Ketty in a way not fitting between a darkie and a white. He decided Ketty was too kept for the fields, so he sent her to the kitchen house to be schooled by the previous cook—who the masa sold some years later as punishment for lying with the breeder he purchased for the women in their years of prime baby-making.

"Lately she's bin disappearing as soon as de masa heads off to town. Et ain't good. She got evvyone in de quarters wondering what she bin up to."

They weren't the only ones. My breathing caught every time the missus said, "Henrietta, I need you to watch Willow. I have things that require my attention." And of course I did what she asked, 'cause she was the missus. I didn't give any lip, and I didn't ask any questions.

When the missus convinced the masa to purchase Mary Grace and me, I was grateful, and I soon came to the understanding that Missus Olivia was unlike my last mistress; she warn't like most white folk. The night I arrived at Livingston, she showed me to the nursery and told me I'd sleep there when the baby came, but until then I would care for her and take on various duties required of a house slave. I'd stood in the middle of the room with Mary Grace fussing in my arms, the front of my shift dripping with milk. Sleeping in the big house so close to the masa's sexual demands petrified me.

She'd placed gentle hands on my shoulders and turned me to face her and lifted my chin, forcing me to look her in the eyes. "As long as you stay close to the house, I can protect you." The seriousness in her gaze unsettled me. "Stay away from Miller, and keep your eyes open."

She went on to say that as long as she was around and I paid heed to her warning, I had nothing to fear. Said Mary Grace and I would be treated right. And she had honored her word. When Miss Willow came I grew to love her like she was my own, and the little miss…she loved me too.

Life in the big house was good, but the days were long and lonely. Folks in the quarters resented us house slaves and, because the missus favored me, the house folk shunned me too. Ketty's love for Missus Olivia allowed her to see me differently. I was drawn to her wisdom and comforted in her attempts to mother me, and she had become my one friend at Livingston.

As isolated as the big house became for me, I observed the same loneliness in the missus. One evening when the masa was off somewhere on his ships, the isolation and stress that afflicted women with their menfolk away had descended on the missus. She had been sitting by the window in the library knitting when her hands paused their work, and she peered at me with tired eyes. "We are friends, aren't we, Henrietta?"

I'd screwed up my eyes, confused by her question. A slave and her mistress, friends? Unsure what to say, I'd continued my dusting like I never heard her. She'd laughed at her own silliness, but from the corner of my eye, I saw the sadness and yearning in her eyes before she dropped her gaze, and the needles began to weave again.

I wanted to make her smile, but I was too scared to admit how much I wished what she spoke of was possible. Because I would wager the missus would be the best of friends. Most days her smiles were reserved for the little miss, and some days she spared one or two for Masa Charles. But it was the times I'd catch her gazing off at some far corner of the room with the prettiest smile on her face that I wondered what memory had occupied her mind.

"Rita, are you listening to me?" Ketty gave my sleeve a jerk.

"Yes."

She put her hands on her hips. "You 'bout to drop from exhaustion. Bin up all night, by de luks of you. De li'l miss needs tending to. Now you best go on inside and do what needs doing."

"I—"

The squeal of children and the stomping of racing

feet stopped my reply. Miss Willow ran through the open doors onto the veranda, with Mary Grace on her heels.

"Mama!" Mary Grace encircled my knees with her chubby arms.

"No, she is Mammy." Miss Willow scowled at Mary Grace before she squeezed me from the other side. I capped each of their heads with a hand, absorbing the love their embrace provided.

Miller rode into the front yard, and my heart felt squeezed. I'd been so caught up in my thoughts and fretting that I'd let my guard down and hadn't noticed him leave the fields. Mary Grace's fingers dug into my leg.

"Lazing around when the master's away, I see. Get back to work," he said, posturing in his saddle, inferring a stature more significant than what met the eye. However, it didn't matter much because, though he sat upon his steed, us womenfolk towered above him from our position on the veranda. And if my knees weren't knocking under my skirt, I would've smirked at his endeavor to be grander than the small man who sat before us.

"Come, Miss Willow. Your pappy and mama be home soon." I wrapped an arm around her shoulders and led her inside.

∽ CHAPTER ∽
Two

MISS WILLOW'S AFTERNOON DRESS LAY IN A HEAP ON the ground, covered with ink after she snuck into her pappy's study while I had my back turned. I slipped the last pearl button through the hole on Miss Willow's dress and set to cleaning her hands the best I could.

Like all children born to wealthy masas, Masa Charles and Missus Olivia insisted the little miss be raised like a proper Southern belle. Educating her in the ways of a lady had started soon after she could walk. Their determination had been rewarded; the little miss could stand up against any of the uppity white folks' children who visited the plantation.

Miss Julia, she had hair the color of hot coals. She was a bubbly child full of spirit. Her personality came from her mama, who Missus Olivia liked a whole lot. Then there was Miss Lucille; she was spoiled in a wrong sort of way—which went beyond the indulgences showered on the white children from their parents. Something warn't right with that one. As for Miss Josephine, the girl was thickly made and tall for her age. She idolized Miss Lucille. I'd catch her mimicking the girl's walk and her mannerisms.

If I were Miss Josephine's mama, I'd keep her away from Miss Lucille.

One afternoon, when Missus Olivia had the girls' mamas over for a luncheon, I'd been in charge of minding the children. I saw Miss Lucille poke a stick through a big old bullfrog like it were nothing, then hold it up for the other girls' inspection, a gleam of pure amusement on her face. *Yes sah, a streak of cruelty run deep in de child.* Little Miss ran to her mama, crying; took the missus and me to calm her down. The missus didn't invite the girl or her mama anymore, and that caused a rift between Missus Olivia and Miss Lucille's mama. Missus Olivia's protectiveness over Little Miss was something fierce. She'd kill for the child; there was no doubt about it. That understanding heightened the kinship I felt toward her.

I turned Miss Willow around and she smiled at me, pleased with our choice of a soft yellow dress. As I smoothed out the layers, my chest got the funny feel that sometimes happened with the girl. *Mammy's white babe is prettier and sweeter den all de others.*

"De masa is back!" a house girl cried from downstairs. The gut feeling chasing me since yesterday plummeted in my stomach.

"Papa!" Miss Willow bolted for the door.

"Wait!" I grabbed for her arm in a desperate attempt to stop her from fleeing.

"Let me go." She twisted and tried to peel my fingers from her arm. "Ow!" Tears puddled in her eyes and one glance at the ivory flesh of her arm revealed the redness imprinted from my tight grip.

I eased my hold. "You can see your pappy soon 'nuf."

Her eyes searched mine for assurance, and she calmed a bit and slipped her hand in mine. "Come, Mary Grace," she said.

Together we walked down the stairs, my steps weighted and lagging. The gnawing voice inside my head grew stronger with each step.

When we reached the veranda, the men and women in the front yard had stopped their tasks. Eyes wild, they turned to bystanders and muttered amongst themselves. In the fields, folks stood upright, their eyes on the lane. Miller whipped the reins of his mount side to side as he rode with urgency toward the big house.

I looked to the lane and spotted the masa walking his horse up the alley, his face drawn and his shoulders slumped. On the back of his horse, a half-naked body of a colored dangled over the horse's rump.

"Henrietta, get Willow inside!" Masa Charles bellowed when he caught sight of us.

"Mama?" Miss Willow grabbed at my skirt, frightened by the sternness in her pappy's voice. "Where's my mama?"

What were you thinking? I scolded myself. The masa could have me punished for my carelessness. I spun on my heel and rushed the children inside. A wide-eyed Ketty met me in the foyer. "Take dem upstairs, I need to…I must…"

"Go. I'll take care of dem," she said. "Come on, chillum, let's go play a li'l game."

"But I don't wanna play a game. I want my mama,"

Miss Willow protested, but Ketty used a firm hand and ushered the girls up the stairs.

I swallowed the lump growing in my throat and hurried back outside. The masa stood beside his horse. "Someone get a blanket and get this girl covered up. Miller," Masa said, "get a grave dug in the slave cemetery. And get a wagon hitched."

"You and you," Miller said to a couple of young men. "Get some shovels." He retrieved the body wrapped in the masa's coat, stumbling under the dead weight and gagging from the smell oozing from the body. A slave man stepped in to help.

"The rest of you get back to work," the masa said, and people darted in every direction.

When they were gone, the masa turned to me as I descended the steps. His boss face faded and he became the fractured man I'd often seen leaving the study after he and Missus Olivia had their fusses about having another baby.

"Masa," I said. "Where's Missus Olivia?"

"Gone." His detachment in the word was haunting.

"Gone?" I said in the same low tone. Panic spasmed through me.

His jaw quivered, but he promptly collected himself and his face stiffened. His eyes fixed on me, and I lowered my gaze. "I'm going back out," he said so quietly I almost missed it. I tilted my ear to hear what he'd say next. "I need you to ask Ketty to gather some food. Hurry, and be discreet."

"Yes, Masa," I turned to head inside, but he stopped me with a hand on my elbow.

"Wait." He ducked his head close to mine. I trembled at his closeness. "I need you to come with me."

"Me, Masa?" I whispered.

"Tell no one what I tell you. I need you to get a dress and shoes from Olivia's armoire, along with things she'd use to freshen up."

Goose pimples invaded the smoothness of my arms. What was the masa wanting those things for? "But—"

"Don't ask questions." His voice quavered in my ear. "Do as I ask and please make it quick." He released my arm, moving away, his gaze flitting over the fields and down the lane like he was scared stiff. I'd never seen the masa in that state, and it terrified me.

I curtsied before hurrying up the path to the front steps and going inside. In the nursery, a tear-stained Little Miss sat cross-legged on the floor, playing with Mary Grace. Ketty squeaked up a racket as she paced the floor, turning her anxious gaze on me when I entered.

She charged right at me, snatched me by the arm, and pulled me to the farthest corner of the room. Glancing at the children, she whispered, "You start talking. Who dat daid girl? And where de missus at?"

"Don't know." Something about how the masa said *gone* troubled me, and his request heightened the inkling haunting me since the missus's disappearance. Where was he fixing to take me, a woman and a house slave?

The sound of the masa's tread on the stairs set my heart to thumping faster. Miss Willow pulled herself to her feet and bounded to the door to fetch him, and I grabbed her on the way by.

She strained away from my hold and wailed, "Papa...I need you."

Masa looked at her and a groan rumbled deep in his chest, then his vacant expression fell on me. "Please see to her. I...I can't."

"Yes, Masa." I shut the door to bar the little miss from running after him.

"I want my mama..." Again the tears came, and my heart ached for the child. Little Miss had always been a sensitive child. Did she sense that something was wrong? I enclosed her in my arms, and she buried her face in the curve of my neck. Her tears dampened the collar of my dress.

"Hush now, angel gal, your mammy be right here." I kissed her dark curls. Mary Grace stood with silent tears slipping over her cheeks at the little miss's distress. "She be all right, Mary Grace. No need to worry. Ketty, go down to de kitchen house and git a sack of food ready. And please take my gal wid ya."

"But why? What is happening?"

"I can't talk 'bout et. And even ef I could, I don't know what I'd be talking about. I know nothin'. Masa said to be quick. You gots to go. I'll see to Miss Willow."

She didn't move.

"Please!" I said with urgency.

"Fine." She took Mary Grace by the hand and gave me another worried look, then opened the door and was gone.

I sat a moment in the rocker with Miss Willow cradled against me, allowing the peacefulness of the nursery to quiet my nerves. Missus Olivia had decorated the room in soft pinks, with a speckle of gold and a little dash of cream here and there. Floor-length curtains rippled in the afternoon breeze whispering through the open windows. Toys aplenty lined shelves. The towering bed sat piled high with pillows, and the little miss had lined up her dolls against them, something she did every morning.

A room befitting a princess, and de li'l miss be jus' dat. I smiled, giving her an extra squeeze.

I glanced down at the child. Oh, how the missus loved her. She and the masa had spoiled Miss Willow something awful. However, I couldn't point all the blame at them; I, too, played a part in her spoiling.

Miss Willow's tears turned to soft whimpers, and I pulled her back so I could look into her eyes. "You's a good gal, Miss Willow. You Mammy's angel gal. Don't you be forgitting et. All right?"

She bobbed her head.

"I got to go wid your pappy for a li'l bit, and while I'm gone, you gwine to stay wid Ketty and Mary Grace down in de kitchen house. But your pappy and I be back 'fore you know et."

"And Mama?" Her face gleamed with hope before her gaze roved over my face in search of an answer.

I didn't know what to say because I didn't hold the answers she sought. And when those answers came, would I want to know?

I heard the masa descend the stairs and I stood, placing the child on the floor. "Now you wipe dose big ol' tears, and I'll take you down to de kitchen house. I got to go git a few things fust, so I need you to stay here."

I hurried down the hallway to the missus's chamber and retrieved the items the masa had ordered before returning to the nursery to grab some toys and the little miss.

We left the big house through the back garden doors. I raced across the work yard, keeping an eye out for Miller and his men.

"Mammy, I can't…" The little miss struggled to keep up with my stride.

"I sorry, angel gal." I bent and pulled her under my arm, half hauling and half carrying her, never slowing my pace until I was safe inside the kitchen house.

When we entered, Ketty was securing kitchen twine around the top of a lumpy potato sack.

"Go play wid Mary Grace." I handed Miss Willow her toys and gave her a gentle nudge. She obeyed and went to sit at the table with Mary Grace.

"Here, I did as you said." Ketty held out the satchel of food.

My hand trembled as I took it from her. "Thank you. Et doesn't luk lak de big house will be needing any supper tonight. See to et you feed Miss Willow and do what et takes to keep her mind off of her pappy and mama."

"Don't you worry none 'bout us, we manage jus' fine." She embraced me and I clung to the warmth of her love before I pulled myself away and hurried to find the masa.

∽ CHAPTER ∽
Three

M ASA DROVE THE WAGON AWAY FROM THE NORTH barn and along the trail leading to the main road. Beside him I sat jostling side to side, the extra weight I'd put on since coming to Livingston offering little protection for my rump against the abuse of the unyielding seat.

The wagon hit a rut and jarred my teeth, but Masa didn't seem to pay it any mind. He stared straight ahead as we rode along, chewing on the inner corner of his mouth—a trait Masa had passed on to his daughter.

Lacking the courage to voice the questions cooking in my head, I remained quiet. When the masa got in his dark ways, we all steered clear of him; even the missus had been leery of his moods. The way she would try to comfort him at times left me puzzled. A look of guilt and shame would overshadow her. Sometimes I found her crying, and when she noticed me she'd quickly dry her eyes and offer me a warm smile. The love between the missus and the masa was fractured, and I had no idea why. Occasionally I found them sealed in a kiss like lovers do, and other times I'd see the masa pacing the floors, looking distraught and tormented while the missus pleaded with him that she was sorry, her face puffy and red from crying.

"She is dead," Masa Charles said, snapping me from my pondering.

"Daid…" I squeaked. Pain knocked me hard in the chest. But…how? Why?

"That slave girl was with her. I found them by the river." Masa turned the wagon down a path barely wide enough for it to fit, and I lifted my arm to shield myself from the thrashing of the branches. "Someone tortured and *used* the girl and…hung them both." Tears clogged his throat. "I've never seen the girl before. What was Olivia doing with her?" He looked at me like a lost boy seeking the guidance of a grown person, and the vulnerability in his eyes frightened me. He couldn't be vulnerable; he was the masa.

"I don't know, Masa," I said, my voice hoarse. "I…I never got a luk at de girl."

Sickness kicked me in the stomach. The missus was gone. How could it be? And the girl…I cringed, remembering the violations by Masa Adams. Memories I desperately tried to forget.

"No one can ever know what happened to her," he said with a long, drawn-out breath.

Keep the missus's death a secret? It didn't make any sense. My concern for the missus beat all common sense clean out of my head and boldness sprang from me before I could yank it back. "How come?"

Gone was the lost man of moments ago. His eyes flashed at my challenging his authority. "Because I said so."

Plain stupidity pushed me forward. I had to know. "Wid your permission, Masa, may I speak frankly?" I said, focusing on the rear end of the horse in front of me.

He sputtered, dumbfounded at my disobedience. In a quick sideways glance, I noticed how his hands pawed and twisted on the reins, causing the horses to jerk their heads and neigh in distress and confusion. "Speak," he said with a grunt.

"Ef someone kilt de missus, we got to tell someone. De slave girl no one is gonna care 'bout besides de loss of money, but de missus, a whole lot of folkses would care. De constable and his men can try to track de ones responsible. Leaving de missus widout justice ain't right. She deserved dat."

They both do, I wanted to say, but masas didn't have any use for opinionated slaves, and I'd given enough opinion already in regards to the missus.

He laughed mockingly; bitterness spewed from him. "Don't you think I want justice? For God's sake, she was my wife. I will not rest until her murderers are dealt with." The conviction in his words led me to believe, despite being but one man, the masa would spend his life chasing the phantom of the murderers, adding to the torment smoldering in him long before I came to Livingston.

"It's not that simple." His whisper echoed with emptiness. The same desolation I'd felt inside when my man lifted his fingers to his lips and pumped his fist to his heart as the wagon carried me away from the Adams plantation.

He didn't want others to know she was dead. Was that why the masa never brought back the missus's body with the slave girl? I knew I couldn't ask any more questions. I kept my lips sealed, but my mind continued spinning.

The farther we got from Livingston, the more scared I became. I hadn't ventured far from the missus's side in over three years, and I certainly hadn't left the plantation.

"Listen," he said. "I'd be blind if I didn't notice the relationship between you and my wife. I know you cared for each other in a way that goes beyond the acceptable relationship between a slave and a master. Olivia always viewed the world in a light I couldn't understand." He continued as if I was his confidant, and inside I squirmed with unease. "But I had no idea how far she had drifted in her beliefs. I have reason to believe she was involved in aiding slaves in escaping."

Escaping? The missus had been kind, but helping slaves to freedom was dangerous. It would explain her disappearances, only to turn up later to slip in the back door, disheveled and eyes panicked. But would she risk everything she loved to help folks like me? The sense of kinship inside me kindled, bringing with it a feeling of significant loss.

Masa Charles rambled on. I listened as slaves were meant to do. Talking to a senseless slave didn't appear as crazy as speaking to oneself would. Masas liked to voice their problems to us; however, they didn't want any response, and it seemed Masa was still trying to figure the situation out in his own head.

The wagon wheel hit a boulder in the path and I was almost launched from the wagon, but the masa snapped me back as quick as nothing. The fabric of my sleeve ripped at the seam. "Hold on," he growled.

Although I was grateful for him saving me from becoming wheel grease for the wagon, I glared at him in my head. *Good thing he handsome, 'cause whatever chewed at him from sunrise to sunset warn't purty.* I gripped the side of the wagon and dug my heels into the floor for extra support. We sat in silence, our bodies left to the mercy of the trail.

I kept my eyes pinned on the trail ahead, too scared of being upended for worries of what was to come to have time to grow. But when the wagon came to a halt some time later, dread quickly overcame my relief.

"Hurry up now. The sun will be setting soon." Masa Charles jumped down and hurried to the back of the wagon. Retrieving two shovels, he disappeared into the trees.

I sprang into action, grabbing the bag of food and the missus's things and dropping to the ground. Not wanting to be left in the woods alone, I ran to catch up.

"Dat you?" I heard a man call out.

"It is," Masa Charles called back. As I caught up, a man stepped out from behind a cluster of trees accompanied by a younger woman and a child. All colored folk. What in heaven's name? The masa never said anything about people hiding in the woods. What was his business with them?

"Here, start digging." Masa Charles tossed a shovel at the man.

The clang of metal hitting rocks rang out as the men struck the earth.

"Henrietta, get some food into the woman and child," Masa said, half winded.

I opened the bag and pulled out some biscuits and smoked meat wrapped in linen cloth and handed the food to them.

"Thank you." The woman took the food and gave some to the child, who mashed it into his mouth, his eyes darting from me to Masa Charles.

After the men had dug a shallow hole, Masa Charles paused, breathless, and rested his forehead on his hands atop the shovel. Observing the tremor in his jaw as he released a deep breath, I choked back the emotions expanding in my chest.

The other man moved to some fallen brush to our right and started lifting branches and tossing them aside, revealing a blanket, a bare foot peeking from beneath it. A low moan rose in my throat as I recognized the feet I'd bathed plenty of times. I put a hand to my mouth to stifle a cry. Grief tunneled through me, ruthless and fierce. It was true; the missus was gone.

Masa stepped up beside the man, and his shoulders sloped forward with defeat and despair. He knelt and lifted the body of the missus into his strong arms and carried it to the opening in the ground. He laid her beside the hole and lifted vacant eyes to me. I knew then why he'd requested I come and bring the missus's things. I nodded my understanding and stepped forward to prepare the body.

The woman and I clothed the missus while the masa and the others stood with their backs turned. After we were done, the woman stood and rejoined the men. Blinded by tears, I combed the missus's hair until it lay in silky layers cascading over her shoulders. My fingers gently touched her cold gray cheek before stroking the burn of the rope on her neck. I would miss her greatly.

My thoughts turned to when Masa Charles had stormed off to England on the day of the little miss's birth. "Promise me you will always care for her, Henrietta," the missus had said through endless tears. "Love her like you do Mary Grace. I'm afraid her lot in life won't be an easy one."

I'd been confused at her request. A child born to the missus and masa would have all the luxuries a child could want, and no shortage of love would fall on the babe. Missus Olivia had a whole lot of love to give, and she'd spent every day singing, reading, and smothering the little miss with affection. And whatever had been bothering Masa that day had faded with time, and he doted on Miss Willow. His undying love surfaced whenever she caught sight of him and called, "Papa"—Masa would break into a rare smile, bend, and extend his arms. Miss Willow would dash into his embrace, and he'd hug her tightly, squashing his love into her little body. The memories of such encounters placed a smile on my heart.

He would've loved the child he'd never have the chance to hold, the babe that lay dead in the missus's womb. The sickness had plagued her most mornings and sometimes late into the afternoon. Her woman business hadn't come last month, but she'd wanted to be sure about the pregnancy before she told the masa. Days after her second missed month passed, the eve before she went missing, she'd sat at her vanity while I combed her hair in preparation for bed. In the looking glass, her gem-like eyes peered at me or through me; I wasn't sure. Her brow furrowed for a moment, then she smiled softly. "I will tell Charles tomorrow."

"Dat is good. De masa be so happy."

"Yes, indeed. He has wanted this for some time."

My hand had paused mid-stroke at the way she said *he*. "And you, Missus?"

"Of course." Her hands had moved to rest on the flatness beneath her white cotton nightgown. "I hope this child will bring healing…" Her thoughts were stolen once again, and silence fell between us.

Bending over her body where it lay in front of me on the ground, I smoothed the wrinkles of the blue muslin fabric of her dress. My fingers paused over her stomach, and the burden of the secret I knew I could never tell unloaded. Tears flowed as I removed the black lace-up boots from the satchel of the missus's things and placed them on her small feet and tied the laces.

I rose to my feet and stepped back. "She ready, Masa."

Leaves rustled as he moved to stand over the body. Soft gasps and weeping cut through the birds singing high in the cypress tree. I stood with the others silently waiting, praying the masa would find the strength to go on for the little miss.

Miss Willow's sweet face sprang into my mind. Runnels of tears fell, and the ache of loss heaved my chest, but I stood upright with my head bowed, sharing in the masa's pain. *How we gonna tell angel gal 'bout dis?* I suppressed a sob. Who'd care for her when the masa was away? With no relatives I was aware of left to care for the child, who'd love her as her mama had?

"I will return," Masa whispered, and retrieved the spades.

After the missus's body lay concealed beneath the earth, the men covered the freshly turned ground with branches. We hid the runaways in the bed of the wagon, and the masa drove us out of the woods and turned in the direction opposite the plantation.

The sun had set below the horizon by the time we reached a small cluster of cabins along the river.

"Stay here," Masa Charles said, tying off the reins. He jumped down and walked to greet an elderly man who exited a cabin and stood waiting on the front stoop. The man stood tall as the evening sky. His skin was dark, but he wasn't like me. I'd never seen someone like him before. Two long silver braids hung over his shoulders, and he wore a shirt and pants of the softest-looking fabric. They exchanged some words, and the man's gaze turned to the wagon.

To my left, a woman stood stirring a large iron kettle over a fire. Her silky raven hair dropped to her waist and hung freely. She eyed me knowingly, as if she knew what I was, then she lifted a hand and waved. I returned the gesture then glanced around, mesmerized by the people of color that roamed the small plantation along the river. Soft chanting of song or prayer came from a man sitting in the dirt in front of a cabin at the farthest end of the plantation. I searched for the overseer, but it seemed the folks were left unguarded.

Soon the masa came back, joined by the elderly man, who gave me the same look as the plantation cook. I listened to the clucking of the man's tongue as it unrolled his words in a strange language. I sat stunned when the masa answered in the same strange chatter. A slender woman approached Masa Charles and held out furs for him to inspect; he cupped her shoulder with a hand and spoke to her in the same language. The newcomer bowed her head, smiled, and strode away.

The men turned back the oilcloth covering the wagon bed. "This is John Bird of the Pee Dee tribe. He'll get you to safety," Masa said to the folks crouched down in the back.

After we left the small plantation on the river, my thoughts returned to the missus and worry stirred in me once more. With the missus dead, what did the future hold for us all?

⚬ CHAPTER ⚬
Four

FEW HOURS BEFORE DAWN, WE SNUCK BACK INTO Livingston by way of the back trail leading to the barn.

"Masa, you go on up to bed, I'll take care of de wagon," I said as he pulled the team of horses to a halt outside of the barn.

The darkness inside of him didn't leave him the strength to fight. He climbed down, opened the barn doors, then turned and ambled toward the big house. I sat for a moment, watching him. Sorrow burrowed through me. What the masa and I had gone through out in the woods tied us together in a way. And my love for the little miss would seal the secret of Missus Olivia's murder.

Glancing down at the reins he'd handed me I realized I didn't know how to drive a wagon, but I reckoned it couldn't be that difficult. I slid over in the seat and flicked the reins and the horses bolted forward, giving my heart a jump. Inside I reined the horses to a stop, relieved at their obedience, climbed down, and lit the lantern hanging on a beam. Unharnessing the horses, I wiped them down, urged them into their stalls, scooped up some feed, and dropped it into their troughs.

"Good boys." I stroked each of their noses. "Guess we all be part of what lies out dere now." The weariness of the past days rushed over me, and I turned to make my way to the big house.

I halted. Fear lurched through me.

Miller.

"Well, if it ain't the pretty little nursemaid." He leaned his shoulder against the doorframe, all casual like, his blue eyes gleaming like he was a cat who'd caught a mouse in its sights.

I desperately looked for an escape. I swung my head back around when I heard his boots scuffing across the straw-laden floor.

"The mister take you out to have a go at you?" he said. "And to think all these years I thought he was too taken with his pretty little wife to bed the slaves." He shook his head and gave a shrug. "Don't matter none to me. With the missus not around to keep you tied up in the house, I suppose you won't be avoiding me tonight." He removed his hat and swiped a hand through his red hair before throwing the hat aside.

I was a tad taller than the man, but his arms were built from long days on the plantation, days when he didn't sit upon his mount barking at the folks toiling on the ground.

Frantic, I darted to the right, but he blocked me. I dodged to the left and felt his fingers grab my arm. I managed to pull free and dashed for the door, but he caught the fabric of my dress and jerked me back. His arm encircled my waist.

I scratched and kicked as he took me into an empty

stall and threw me to the ground. Pain throbbed through my head as it cracked against something solid, knocking me senseless for a moment. The sound of Miller undoing his trousers returned my focus. I struggled to sit up, and my hands felt the cold hard object that had connected with my head and now lay in the straw beside me. My fingers tightened around the metal tine of a pitchfork, and I quickly grabbed for the handle as Miller advanced to hover over me. The odor of the onions he ate like apples snatched my breath away.

Fear clawed at me. "Stay away!" I lifted the pitchfork, blindly jabbing it in front of me.

His laughter echoed. "And what are you going to do?" He swatted at the pitchfork, trying to capture it, but I drew it back, clutching it tightly as I scrambled to get to my feet.

He inched closer and leaped at me. Panicked, I thrust the pitchfork again, and it met something forcefully. A harrowing groan sounded, and I froze as weight pressed on the end of the fork.

My gaze flew to Miller and fear squeezed my chest. The overseer stood before me, a look of horror and pain gripping his face. "Y-you stabbed me!" he croaked, his hands clutching his stomach. Blood oozed, soaking his shirt where the pitchfork had pierced him. "You'll h-hang...for this." Alarm leaped into his eyes, and he fell forward. The pitchfork twisted his body on impact, pinning me under his dead weight.

I stared into his blank eyes, gagging on his foul scent. I kicked and shoved, trying to get his body off of me. Rolling to the side, I pushed him from me and clambered to my feet. A warmth penetrated the bodice of my dress, and I looked down to see the crimson liquid painting the front of me. Frantically, I tried to wipe away the evidence of what I'd done. I held my hands in front of me, peering at his blood staining them before I was drawn to the lifeless body sprawling in the straw.

Lard help me. I kilt him! Tears burned my eyes. It was the end of me. *Mary Grace...*A groan filled my chest. What would happen to her? *What have I done! I didn't mean to... I...I was only trying to...* The defense forming in my mind halted. It didn't matter what I was trying to do; I was a slave, and I'd killed a white man.

I'd spent all my days at Livingston avoiding being caught alone with a man. Finding any excuse to exit a room or turn and rush down the corridor when the masa came into view. When I had no choice but to leave the security of the big house and spotted Miller or his men coming, I'd dash between buildings to keep from being seen. With time the fear of men's whims became less daunting. The masa had no interest in me, and the missus had become my protector. But all that was gone now.

"Miller, you in here?" a man called out.

I dropped to the floor, holding my breath at the sound of Miller's man.

"Miller," he said again.

A horse neighed in the stall next to me and stomped its hoof, threatening to give me away. I squeezed my eyes shut, curling into the darkened corner of the stall, praying for him to leave. As the silent prayer moved my lips, I stopped. I had no right to ask God for protection. Not after the unforgivable sin I'd committed. I was alone. No one could help me now, and a vast emptiness befell me.

The man mumbled something I couldn't catch and the lantern went out, plunging me into darkness. I heard him close the barn doors and bar them. Tears escaped me as I sat with my knees drawn up to my chest, my arms pulled tight around them. I rocked back and forth as grief and fear coursed through me.

Minutes passed before I pulled myself together and began trying to figure out what I was going to do. I paced the barn, considering my options.

I could get Ketty to help me bury the body, but with her frailty I doubted we'd be able to handle the task alone. Besides, involving her would only endanger us both. No, I couldn't enlist her help. I ran through a list of faces on the plantation and came up with the same answer: it was useless, I had no one. If the missus had been alive I might have enlisted her help, but considering the impossible wouldn't solve my problem.

Then a face came to mind. Could I? No. My heart raced faster. I had no choice, I had to try. I hurried to the side door and breathed a sigh of relief to find it not locked from the outside. Slipping out into the night, I glanced around. Seeing no one, I darted for the house. Avoiding going in through the work yard, I went around the house to the front and climbed the steps to the front veranda. I opened the door and stepped inside. Darkness had engulfed the house and it lay silent, with the house staff retired for the night.

A low flicker of light drew my gaze down the

corridor to the study. Was the masa still up? I crept down the hallway and paused outside the open door of the study. Peeking around the doorframe, I saw him sitting hunched over the desk, his eyes blank and staring at nothing in particular.

A floorboard creaked under my feet, and his gaze turned to the doorway. "Did you manage to take care of the team?"

"Yes, Masa."

"Then, please, relieve Ketty of her watch. Willow will need you now more than ever."

"I love de li'l miss, and I take care of her as you ask. But..."

"But what?" Weariness echoed in his voice as he pulled himself to his feet.

I stepped into the room and closed the door behind me. My hand on the knob, I squeezed my eyes tight and summoned up the courage I was afraid I didn't possess. The courage to tell the masa that I'd killed his overseer.

"What in heaven's name are you doing?" he said.

I turned as he came to stand a few feet from me, his brow dipping in confusion. "Masa." I rubbed my hands over the blood marring the front of my dress. "Somepin' dreadful has happened. I didn't mean—"

"Is that blood on your dress?" His voice hitched.

"Yes."

"Whose?"

"Miller's."

"What in tarnation do you mean? How could—"

"Et was a mistake. He came at me when I was

tending to de horses. He tried…well, he tried to take me, and I panicked."

"Panicked? Where is he now?"

"Where I left him, in de horse stall."

"This attack can't go unpunished." His voice remained a whisper. "He'll want justice. I can't be viewed as a nigger lover, or all is lost. They killed my wife for her beliefs. Who is next, my daughter? No. You must step up and face your punishment."

"But, he daid, Masa."

"Dead? What do you mean?" he said through clenched teeth. He grabbed me by the shoulders and gave me a rough shake. "Out with it, Henrietta."

Tears came in floods. "I reached for anything I could to keep him back. I grabbed a pitchfork and jabbed et at him. Et was an accident; I didn't mean to kill him."

Stumbling back, his eyes wide with horror and disbelief, he lifted a hand and pulled it over his face. "Lord help us all." He dropped like a deadweight into the brown leather chair in front of his desk, fear and bewilderment rippling over his face.

I stood rooted, my hands knotting the skirt of my dress, unsure what to do or say that would make the mess I was in any better.

When his attention turned back to me, several minutes had passed. He rose and closed the distance between us.

In a low tone, he said, "You'll tell no one of this. Get upstairs and get out of those clothes, burn them, and get into bed. I'll take care of this."

"But Masa, what you gwine to do?"

"Bury him far away from here. And then I've no choice but to set things into motion."

My mouth went dry. "What things?" I wanted to say, but I knew better than to ask because at that moment I feared the wrath of Masa Charles more than facing the noose or damnation for murdering a man.

"Now go. And make sure no one sees you."

I nodded, turned to the door, opened it, and hurried from the room.

Ketty lay asleep in a rocker she'd drawn up beside the little miss. Snores loud enough to rattle the windowpanes vibrated throughout the nursery. Dim light glowed from a lantern on the stand by the floor-length looking glass in the far corner of the room. I tiptoed to the closet and removed my night shift, tucked into the back of the closet. Standing before the mirror, I undid the front buttons of my dress and wiggled out of it, letting it pool in a heap on the floor. Ketty's snoring ceased, and my heart skipped. When her sleeping melody rang out again, I breathed and turned back to the glass.

Studying my body in the reflection, I barely recognized myself anymore. Thickness from extra helpings of food in the big house had served as a shield, transforming the curves that encouraged the lust of men like Masa Adams into soft folds of fat. However, my shield had done nothing to keep Miller at bay. After slipping the night shift over my head, I collected my dress and trudged down the back stairs to wash away the blood marring my face and hands.

Later I lay on my pallet at the foot of the little miss's bed, nestled against Mary Grace's warm body. I breathed in the scent of her hair and kissed her head. "Et all gonna be fine," I whispered into the darkness of the room. My chest heaved and tears spilled, disappearing into the softness of my daughter's hair. How was I going to figure this mess out? I cried harder, until sobs racked my body.

I'd heard the masa's horse ride out when I stood watching the flames of the fire in the parlor chew through my bloodstained dress. The gulps of the masa's whiskey I'd snuck scarcely relieved the guilt I harbored inside me. I waited for his return until I couldn't withstand the exhaustion pulling at my eyelids any longer, and I surrendered to the world of dreams often ruled by nightmares.

๑ CHAPTER ๑
Five

S OMETIME DURING THE NIGHT, THE LITTLE MISS HAD FOUND her way to Mary Grace's and my pallet. I awoke as the house slaves begin to stir to find her pressed up behind me, her hand clutching the fabric of my shift. For a short, greedy minute, I lay in the sweet, warm swaddling of the girls and everything was as it used to be. Any minute now I'd hear the missus leave her room and amble downstairs to make herself a coffee, then she'd wander out to the veranda and I'd hear the squeak of the porch swing. All the horrors of the last days would vanish, and all would be right in the big house again.

If only it could be so.

I slipped from the children's grasp and sat up. The gravity of all that was wrong in my world lodged on my shoulders, and I pulled my knees to my chest and rested my cheek on them. What I wouldn't do to rewind time. I would try to stop the missus from leaving that morning, and maybe if I'd let Miller use my body…I expelled a sigh, blocking the thought from my mind.

I quietly dressed before exiting the room and slipping down the back stairway.

The front double doors of the house lay open and

Masa's manservant, Thaddeus, stood sweeping the dirt and leaves from the veranda. Masa mounted the steps, stiff with exhaustion. "See that someone tends to my horse."

"Yes, Masa." Thaddeus bounded down the steps to retrieve the horse.

After Thaddeus disappeared, the masa removed his hat and stood in the foyer, staring down at his hands as if the body he'd disposed of the previous night had died at his hands. Guilt raked its talons over my soul, but I pushed it back and hurried to greet the masa.

Glancing around to make sure we weren't overheard, I said, "Is he—"

He lifted a hand. "I'm going to my chambers. See to it I'm not disturbed."

"But—" He sent me a warning glare. "Yes, Masa." I bowed my head.

The sound of his boots faded down the corridor. Gathering my composure, I tipped my head around the staircase banister, peering after him. He walked into his study, and soon reappeared with a bottle of whiskey in his hand. He strode past me without so much as a sideways glance and wearily ascended the stairs without another word.

The guilt inside of me nagged. Had the man not been through enough? If I'd let Miller do his business, Masa wouldn't have another secret to add to those multiplying between us.

"Morning, Rita," Ketty said from behind me.

I jumped, instinctively lifting balled hands to hold off an enemy.

"What has gotten into you, gal?" She stood stunned, a line carved between her brows. "Evvything all right?"

I swept my hands through the air. "Does et luk lak evvything be all right?"

"Still no word on de missus?"

The evidence of a sleepless night pulled at her features. A wave of tenderness swept over me; I'd been so busy helping the masa hide the missus's murder and being caught up with worrying about the killing he covered up for me that I hadn't given consideration to what Ketty may be suffering. After all, she too loved the missus.

"Shh!" I grabbed her elbow and led her from the house out onto the veranda.

"What dis all 'bout?"

"De masa said he warn't to be disturbed. He ain't bin sleeping much. Worried sick, I'd gather," I whispered.

"Where he off to so early dis morning? Heard him jus' come back."

"Out searching for de missus."

"She always wandering off. When she was a li'l gal, she went missing for hours. She'd gotten herself lost after she chased off after a mama deer and her babe. Masa Shaw and de missus were beside demselves wid worry, thinking she'd wandered into de swamps and become prey to de low country critters. Dat incident took de adventure outta her for a while, but den when she got older et was lak she forgot all 'bout dat time."

I thought of the insects and dirt critters climbing over the missus's body under the earth. *Et ain't right! She should be buried right here at Livingston. She loved dis place.*

"Rita!" Ketty snapped her fingers in my face.

"What!" I said louder than intended. My nerves hadn't stopped zapping since the missus had gone missing.

"We gots to find her." Tears fractured her voice.

"And how you 'pect we do dat? Take a wagon and go out ourselves? What can we do dat de masa ain't already done? We slaves; we wouldn't get past de gate 'fore dey drag us back."

"What we gonna do, wid de missus missing and de masa beside himself wid worry? Holing up in his room ain't gonna help no one. Dat leaves Miller to run de place, and he 'bout as evil as dey come."

Missus Olivia had loathed Miller as much as the rest of us. She'd begged Masa Charles to get rid of him, but he said he needed a firm hand to run the place in his absence. She'd intervened on more than one occasion when Miller got to beating slaves nearly to death. Upon Masa Charles's return, Miller would snitch like the slimy weasel he was, and Masa would get awfully mad at the missus, said she was overstepping her authority. But I believed the love he held for Missus Olivia lessened the severity of his reaction, and he didn't strike her like I'd seen Masa Adams do to his wife.

"We gonna help run dis place."

She scoffed, "Dat's why de white folkses got demselves overseers. Ain't no coloreds ever run a plantation 'fore."

"'Round midnight I saw Miller slip on out of here. Ain't saw him come back, either. Maybe he de one responsible for de missus's disappearance." The smoothness of my lie added to the troubled feeling swirling around inside me since the accident.

"What you saying? Dat Miller done away wid de missus?"

"Maybe." I shivered, imagining Miller's eyes on me from the grave. "He missing and she missing. You know how he lusts for women."

"Masa got a temper to watch out for. Nobody dare cross him. Yes, sah. He'd shoot Miller daid ef he got a harebrained idea lak dat."

I almost said, "Ain't got to worry 'bout dat now, do he?" but caught myself in time.

"No one messes wid Missus Olivia and gits away wid it. You see," her voice lowered, "Missus Olivia was in love wid another man 'fore Masa Charles."

"Another?" The missus had never mentioned another man.

"Dat right. She was in love wid Masa Charles's younger brother, Masa Ben. She used to tell me dey were gwine to marry and run off to a place called Europe. See de world together." Fondness glimmered in her hazel eyes. "Adventure run deep in dat one's blood. But wid Missus Shaw daid and Masa Shaw sickly, her pappy started luking for a husband for his gal. Didn't want her left wid no one. De Hendricks brothers had a small family too, jus' de two boys. Deir pa wasn't de same when he came back from de war, and deir ma had died while he was away—leaving Masa Charles, de older son, to care for Masa Ben. De brothers and Missus's pappies were friends since dey were boys, and deir chillum grew up together.

Dere was always talk of de missus marrying one of dem. So when Masa Shaw luked for a husband for his gal, he decided on Masa Charles, because Masa Ben was young and in some fancy doctor school."

"Where he now?"

"Took off soon after Masa Charles and Missus Olivia married. Some slaves say Masa run him off," she said. "Maybe she finally ran off to find him."

"Oh, hush. De missus never leave her babe for no man," I said. I didn't take to anyone speaking of the missus like she was impure. "All right, 'nuf 'bout what we don't know. Dere tasks dat need doing. I'll bring de li'l miss down to de kitchen house to eat her breakfast."

"Now I knowed you lost your mind. De masa won't be wanting Miss Willow eating in de kitchen house."

"Masa said no one is to disturb him and dat is what we gwine to do. We let him sleep and go 'bout our work."

"Have et your way. You know where I be." She turned on her heels and marched down the stairs with surprising spryness for a woman of her years.

Thaddeus had returned and had taken up his sweeping. "Masa is tired and requested not to be disturbed. You see dat no one comes in and out of de house unless dey be house slaves," I told him.

"And he left you in charge?" He arched a silver-threaded brow.

"Well…no."

"Down at the stables, they're saying that Miller's missing."

My blood pulsed in my ears and a lie raced from my tongue. "Heard him ride out late last night."

He studied me suspiciously. "How strange," he said in his customary white-speaking way. Ketty said Thaddeus was the son of a masa and his pappy taught him the King's proper English. His pappy's wife hated Thaddeus and his mama, 'cause she bore her husband lots of children. But his pappy favored him most of all. Took him around in his carriage, dressed up in smart-looking clothes, like he was a child born of his wife. When that masa died, his wife sold Thaddeus and his family in New Orleans, where slave traders dressed slaves up in lavish clothing and makeup, staging them as presentable and of good health for purchasers.

I eyed the man before me. Handsome darkie he was, dressed head to toe in a tailored suit and white gloves. But the fancy attire didn't conceal the stiffness in his right leg. Folks said he'd become a runner when his last masa put him in the fields; he warn't used to the harshness of long days in the fields. Last masa sold him because he tired of chasing him down. No punishment could stop him from trying to flee to search for his family. I admired the courage of a man like him. Yet now, with the overseer gone and the masa passed out drunk, he never took the opportunity. Maybe Davis, Miller's right-hand man, and the driver, Winston, scared him into staying. Lord knows they weren't that much different from Miller.

"Lots of funny business gwine on 'round here." I busied myself with straightening a rocker to avoid his keen stare. "But et ain't our business to be saying nothin'.

When de masa's up, he do all de figuring. In de meantime, we do what slaves do and take care of dis place."

"You're a bossy one," he said with a shake of his head.

I opened my mouth to reply, but Miss Willow's soft call came from somewhere in the house, and I pushed past Thaddeus and went inside.

Miss Willow stood at the top of the stairs in her cotton nightgown, her dark ringlets tousled and matted from yet another restless sleep.

"What is et, angel gal?" I gathered the sides of my skirt and hurried up the stairs, crouching low on the top step. From down the hall, the masa's snores sounded.

"I'm hungry." She pushed a lock of hair from her eyes.

"Let's git you dressed and den we go down and see Ketty in de kitchen house." I led her back down the hall to the nursery.

Mary Grace sat on the pallet, sleep still heavy in her eyes. A lazy smile spread on her face when she saw Miss Willow and me. House folks's children were sent to the plantation nursery to be raised down there, but the missus wouldn't allow the masa to separate me from my girl. And, because of her, every day I woke to the comfort of Mary Grace's body next to mine, and each day I whispered a prayer of gratitude that the missus had chosen me.

"Morning, chile." I leaned down and kissed her cheek.

Miss Willow dropped to her knees beside my girl. "Mammy says we gonna eat in the kitchen house." Excitement lit her pretty green eyes. "What you think of that, Mary Grace?"

Mary Grace smiled in the contented, kind of way of

a child. No concern, no worries. And I intended to keep it that way.

"Come, let's git you both dressed," I said.

Dressed and wearing smiles bright as polished silver, the babes followed me down the stairs, out the slave entrance, and across the work yard to the kitchen house.

Once the girls were seated at the table in front of the hearth, Ketty put a plate of hot cakes and sausages in front of them. I gasped and reached for the plate in front of my daughter, who sat staring at it in awe. "Ketty!" I scolded. "You know we ain't supposed to be eating de food of de masas."

"And who gwine to know?" She grabbed the plate back and set it down in front of Mary Grace. "Eat, and make et quick." She placed a hand on Mary Grace's shoulder, her eyes planted on me—challenging-like.

"Someone luking to find favor in de white men's eyes."

She took my hand and led me to the far corner of the small room. Lowering her voice, she said, "Snitching niggers be lower den Miller's kind." Her face twisted with disgust. "Lak dat driver, Winston. He be as black as us, but he has de heart of de whites. Thinks nothin' of beating his own kind. Folkses knows he forces himself on de women. Caught a luk at dat purty gal Masa Charles purchased a few years back when she was washing. Bruises marked her body front and back. Someone took at her. When I asked her she wouldn't say, but when Winston walked by, she trembled lak a heifer giving birth."

Nausea roiled in me at the thought of what the girl

may have suffered. I remembered the day she arrived at Livingston, soon after my arrival. I'd come out on the back veranda when the masa had driven the wagon around back. The caramel-skinned girl had hunkered down in the corner of the wagon bed, her eyes flitting around with anxiety and fear as she took in her new home. Soon I'd come to understand she was bought as a breeder, but she was a purchase that wouldn't bring a profit, as she had never borne any children.

My thoughts turned to my four-year-old daughter; Mary Grace had the same beautiful shade of skin as the breeder girl. Mulatto girls fetched a large sum at the market because the white men loved them. The ever-troubling need to shield her from horrors the young woman and I had suffered mounted in me. With poor Missus Olivia dead, there was no one to step in if someone came after us. But that was the last thing I could fret about, because what had happened in the barn exceeded all my other problems. Would the masa turn me over to the frenzy of the hate mob? I'd heard what they'd done to Mr. Carter's slave after he slaughtered his masa's hog to feed his starving family before running off. Folks said he wasn't the same in the head since. I shuddered at the thought.

"Rita?" Ketty laid her hand on my arm. "You luk far away. Lak somepin' snatched your mind."

"Worried, is all."

"'Bout de missus?"

I nodded. "And all of us. Missus Olivia cared for us in a way Masa Charles never would. She did her best to help us."

"She always was a good gal. Pure of heart. She de light in dis place." She lifted the hem of her apron and picked at the seam. "Can't sleep or eat, worrying 'bout what happened to her."

I wanted to ease her mind and tell her Missus Olivia was dead. Maybe then she could find some peace. But I knew what I desired was impossible. Masa said no one could know the truth.

She turned from me, brushing away falling tears, and lifted a knife and began chopping vegetables for the evening meal. I couldn't bear to see her fret, so I gathered the girls, kissed Ketty's cheek, and left the kitchen house.

CHAPTER Six

MASA CHARLES LAY PASSED OUT FOR THE GOOD PART of a week, only leaving his room to return moments later with another bottle of whiskey. Each day I set a tray of food outside his door, and each day it remained untouched.

I worried what friends and neighbors were going to say of the masa if he didn't find it within himself to exist in a life he no longer desired to be part of. I'd listened in on social gatherings hosted by the masa and missus, and though the folks of Charleston prided themselves on being God-fearing folk, their abundant churches and talk of faith couldn't blot out their loathing and common belief that my kind were like animals without souls. No matter what the Good Book states, they twisted its words for their own personal gain. The masa was right; their tongues would wag, and if they found out about the missus's doings, Livingston and the family would suffer.

As days melded together, my growing concern reflected on Thaddeus's face and scattered throughout the plantation. Some of the slaves ran off, and the white workers of the estate went out looking for them. They returned some time later with a few of the runaways, but while they were out hunting others took their leave and ran off. The runaways caught were punished as Masa Shaw had done while he'd been alive: a brand of a cross was burned into the middle of their forehead, warning others they were runaways. Second offenders had their ears cropped. One man whom slaves had named Dimwit Johnny had been fool enough to try a third time, and with Masa Charles indisposed, Winston and Davis severed his hamstring. Dimwit Johnny wouldn't run anymore, and if he were dumb enough to try, he'd not make it far before the hounds would chase him down.

They'd strapped a man to the whipping post, and each crack of the whip drew forth agonizing cries. I sat in the library with Mary Grace and Miss Willow on my lap, their faces buried in my bosom, tears dampening my blouse. Anger surged in me. It was time for the masa to drag himself out of that bed and get control of his place.

Miss Willow's hands muffed her ears, and her sobs grew louder. "Stop. Stop. Stop."

The house folks jumped at the sound of each lash, and worried eyes turned to the windows overlooking the work yard. Some huddled in corners, whispering, looking at the little miss like she was the cause of all that was happening.

Something snapped in me, and I rose to my feet and sat the girls on the settee. "Thaddeus," I called out.

"Yes, Miss Rita."

"Stay wid de girls. I'm gwine to git de masa." I strode by him, but he seized my arm and hauled me back.

"I wouldn't do that if I were you."

"He can't stay in dat bed. He's got to git up and run dis place or et will be de end of us all." I jerked my arm free and hurried from the room before I lost my courage.

Outside the masa's door, I took a deep breath before knocking. Lightly at first, but when no reply came, I pounded harder. "Masa?"

A mumble came from within, and I waited. Nothing.

"Masa, we need you out here."

Movement sounded within, and then a faint call echoed back. "Go away."

The sound of the man pinged my nerves, and the boldness I displayed next came from years spent being spoiled by the missus—like her, I forgot my place.

Gripping the brass knob, I turned it and pushed open the door. I was greeted with the stench of alcohol and the masa's unwashed body. The heavy, green velvet curtains were drawn, plunging the room into darkness. I strode to the window and pulled back the curtains, and the sunlight of a beautiful day, tainted by what was unfolding around me, seeped across the room.

"What in the blazes!" Masa Charles placed a forearm over his eyes to ward off the light. "Who dares enter my chambers?"

"Et's me, Masa." I curtsied.

"Henrietta, I told you I wasn't to be disturbed."

I kept my eyes downcast, but even the harsh pounding of my heart didn't stop me. "But Masa, we need you. Widout you and wid no overseer, de plantation is fallin' apart. Slaves run off, and de white men are freely unleashing punishments. No mussy is shown. Fust dey took to whipping jus' de runaways, but now dey takin' to whipping folkses for no reason at all."

He grumbled, and his legs dropped over the side of the bed as he sat up. Groaning, he placed a hand to his forehead before he turned his attention to the commotion outside. "What's the slave's crime?" He rose and walked to the window overlooking the work yard.

"Accused of not showing up in de fields on time. His wife gave birth early dis mornin' and, well, she didn't make et. Died widdin an hour of de chile's birth. De man was beside himself wid grief."

Another grumble came from the masa. "Have Thaddeus sent up to attend me. And you go down and tell those imbeciles I said enough."

"Me, Masa? But I'm jus' a house slave."

He spun around, his face resembling that of a snorting bull. "Do you wish to see the slave beaten to death?"

"No, Masa."

"Well, I can hardly go down there looking like this. Now go!"

I fled the room and bounded down the narrow staircase.

"Sooky," I called to the woman scrubbing the floors. "I need you to mind de chillum."

"Yes, Miss Rita." She dropped her rag into the pail of water and pulled herself to her feet.

"Thaddeus, de masa wants you upstairs, and make et quick. Masa's gonna set things right here."

I spun and raced out the back door. A wail rose as Winston unleashed another blow on the man whose fist clutched the ropes binding his wrist to the whipping post. I wove my way through the cluster of folks rounded up and forced to watch the man's punishment—white peoples' reminder to us all that if we stepped out of line, our fate would be the same.

Davis stood back with his arms folded across his chest, pleasure gleaming on his whiskered face as he observed the beating.

"Sah, Masa says to stop," I said, my words barely a mumble. I tried again, but the words stuck in the dryness of my throat. I clenched my hands at my sides and bellowed, "Stop!"

Winston's hand froze in midair, and he spun to look at the slaves.

Davis dropped his arms, his face twisting as his guttural roar plunged fear into us all. "Who dared breathe an order?"

The folks on either side of me kept their heads down. No one spoke, and only the soft groans of the injured man slumped against the post could be heard.

"Speak up!" Gravel scratched under his feet as he circled the ground in front of us.

My heart thudded behind my breastbone—harder, faster. I crept forward. "I did." I kept my eyes fastened on the ground.

"You?"

"Masa Charles sent me to tell you to stop dis punishment right now." My voice grew louder.

He laughed. "And why would he send a slave to do a master's work?"

"Because he got important matters he is attending to. But he said you be next ef you don't follow his orders," I lied—an ugly habit that seemed to be coming easier by the day.

"Did he now?" Winston moved closer to me.

"Mighty big words for a man without an overseer who seems to have resigned himself to hiding within the walls of his home," Davis said, finding courage in the withdrawal of the masa. Masa Charles had to pull himself out of the pits of despair he'd climbed into, or men like Davis would stir a rebellion against him.

"He come, and you be sorry." I ground my heels into the dirt, fighting to hold onto the courage I had scarcely mustered.

"I don't believe you. I think you're trying to step in 'cause you skeered. Maybe you de nigger who should be tied to dis post." Winston's hot breath warmed my cheek.

I looked him straight in the eye. His black eyes mirrored the evil spun so tight inside of him. We all despised him as much, or more than, we did Miller and his men. But that was the whites' intent; they strove to hammer a wedge between Winston and us, giving a colored a position to rule over us, ensuring we hated him. If I wasn't aware of the darkness coiled inside of him and the horrors he had unleashed on us, I might have felt sorry for the man. However, he was a man filled with as much hostility and dislike for us as the whites.

Davis stepped forward. "You untie him and let's show this delicate little house slave who is in charge."

"No!" I cried as Winston grabbed my arm, pinning it behind me. "De masa sent me. I swear et."

A blow to the mouth silenced my protest. My mouth burned with pain, and warm wetness trickled over my bottom lip and down my chin.

Hands grabbed at the back of my dress, tearing away the fabric, and cool air touched my bare flesh. Winston and Davis wiggled my upper body from the dress, and I stood exposed.

"You men stop dis right now!" The sound of Ketty's voice heightened the fear storming through me, and I felt the gentle touch of her hand on my shoulder.

"Ketty, no…" I moaned.

Her voice quivered, but she wouldn't back down. "Ef she say de masa sent her, den she telling de truth."

"It seems to me we have another one looking to be disobedient in the absence of the master. Ain't that so, Winston?"

"Sure seems dat way." Winston grinned, his inky eyes flickering with the appetite for blood.

Davis planted a boot square in the center of Kitty's chest, sending her sailing backward.

"No!" I pulled at Winston's grip as Ketty hit the ground with a bone-cracking thud. She screeched, pain rippling over her face.

A murmur sliced through the circle of slaves.

"Stay down ef you know what's good for you," Winston spat in her direction before swerving back to the slave tied to the whipping post. He bent and removed the rope from the man, who crumpled to the dirt, nearly dead. Bending, Winston tossed him to the side, discarding him like one of the bodies thrown into wagons after yellow fever tore through the quarters in the heat of the summer.

"Get her tied up." Davis shoved me into Winston's arms.

No, please help me.

Tied to the post, I looked to the masa's chamber window, willing him to come to my rescue. And then I saw him standing there, looking down at us, stunned and unmoving.

Masa, please, my soul cried out, believing that there was goodness deep inside of him somewhere, the goodness a woman like the missus had seen, deeming Masa Charles a man worthy of love.

The first blow of the whip buckled my legs. I screamed as unimaginable pain ripped through my body. Never had a strap touched my flesh; the shock sent my body into spasms. I pulled at the ropes, trying to stand up, hiding my face to avoid being snagged by the tip of the whip.

The whip came again, this time harder. And the scream that burst from me sounded foreign to my own ears.

"Mammy!" In the distance, Miss Willow's wail broke through the pain.

Angel gal… My heart ached. I braced for the next lash, gritting my teeth to keep from crying out.

"Stop!" Masa bellowed.

"Mr. Hendricks, sir, this slave was out of line," Davis said.

"She was obeying my orders."

"I…I thought—"

"Silence! Winston, cut her down. Ketty, find someone capable of taking over your duties. You're to care for my daughter until Henrietta is fit to return to her duties."

"Right away, Masa." Ketty's voice was thick with tears.

The pull of the ropes securing me eased, and I slumped to the ground, my face resting against the post. A low moan escaped me.

"The rest of you get back to work. If I hear of any more of you running off, I'll hang you myself. Now go!"

When the thud of scurrying footsteps ceased, the masa spoke again. "Winston, you better make yourself scarce before I drag you through this yard tied to the back of my horse."

"I was following orders," Winston said, allowing all the blame to fall on Davis.

From beneath half-closed lids, I peered up at the men. Winston stood with his shoulders hunched forward, and Davis kicked at the dirt with his boot.

The tendons in Masa's neck corded, and his nostrils flared. "I'm no fool. I know you enjoyed this stint of power as much as Davis. I ought to take the price of your disregard for my property out of both of your hides."

"But Mr. Hendricks—" Davis started.

Masa stopped him with, "Go, both of you!"

When they were gone, the masa turned and bent to lift me into his arms. I groaned from the pain, biting my lip to quiet a cry. "I should never have sent you," he said as he began to walk. "All of this is my fault. Olivia would never forgive me for letting this happen to you."

"Ain't your fault," I whispered. "You hurting."

He grimaced but spoke no more.

He carried me to the plantation's hospital. The doc who stayed on year-round to care for the masa and his family came to stand on the front stoop. Masa Charles took me inside and deposited me facedown on a cot. He conversed with the doctor, leaving instructions that I was to receive the same care a member of his own household would before he stormed out the door, slamming it behind him.

ᦀ CHAPTER ᦀ
Seven

D AYS SPENT IN THE SICK HOSPITAL BLENDED TOGETHER.
Sweat stuck my shift to me like skin as pain
erupted through my body. My hands knotted
the bed linens, and I called out for Big John. A cold, damp
cloth blotted my forehead, and a woman's soothing voice
broke through the fog of the hallucinations.

"I didn't mean to," I cried. "Et was an accident."

"What's she talking about?" a man said.

"Et ain't nothin'. De fever done caught her mind, is
all."

Ketty? I'm sorry. So sorry. My silent plea echoed in my
head.

Then I saw Miller hovering over me. "Murderer!" he
screamed. His belly gaped open, and blood gushed from
the pitchfork wound.

Stay away from me! I started thrashing on the cot. The
pain snatched my breath away.

The man's voice came again. "Hold her down. She'll
open her wounds. I'll give her something to calm her."

I don't know how many hours or days passed before
my eyes fluttered open and I was alone in the darkness of
the one-room hospital. The moon spied on me from its

seat in the black-and-gray-marbled night. I imagined my girl asleep on her pallet, alone and missing her mama. I ached to hold her and smell her hair and hear the tranquility of her light breathing. Then I recalled the night Big John and I had become husband and wife under the stars. After our lovemaking, we'd lain in the grass and he'd spoken of his homeland, where he was ruler over his people—a land where he was admired and respected as a man of greatness. The pain of his absence from my life never ceased. I used to pray every night that one day we'd be reunited.

Since the night in the barn, I didn't pray anymore. The Mighty One didn't shine favor on people like me. I'd broken one of His commandments, and for that He wouldn't hold any place for me in His kingdom.

The hallucinations faded as my body started to heal, and I became aware of my surroundings. I was alert when the slave folk came to gawk through the windows; the thin glass offered little shelter from their brash ridicule.

"Always was de missus's chosen pet," the weaver woman said.

"Probably taken up wid de masa now, to git dis kind of treatment," another said, her breath steaming the window.

Despite the burning from the stretching of freshly fused wounds, I turned my back to them. Hot tears trickled down my cheeks and caressed my neck. The guilt of being a kept slave by the missus shadowed me. I had witnessed the horrors unfurled on the others while I cowered behind the protection of the missus, but the fear of knowing what happened to women deemed pretty kept me quiet. I had protected my own no matter the chastisement I'd received over the years, obtaining safety for Mary Grace and myself in a life with no certainty. Death would greet me first before I would allow anyone to hurt my child. Security, as much as a slave could find, had found me within the walls of the big house. The world I knew outside of Livingston was a place to which I wouldn't return. I'd wagered my soul to warrant this and for what? My assurance lay dead in a hidden grave in the woods.

I was on the mend the evening Ketty came to visit me with Mary Grace in tow, bringing word that the little miss was distraught and asking for me.

"I gotta git out of dis bed." I used my elbows to prop myself up, gasping from the immediate burn threading over my back.

"Easy." Ketty placed a hand on my shoulder. "Your wounds are barely closed. You won't do anyone any good ef you have to stay here longer 'cause you too damn stubborn to rest while you gots de chance."

I halted my protest and clamped my lips tight. When Ketty used profanity, most folks had the common sense not to cross her because she was about a snail's length away from losing her temper. Although she didn't weigh more than a newly sprouted sapling, she went all crazy-eyed and started cussing up enough of a racket to put the fear of God into any heathen.

Mary Grace sat beside me on the small cot holding my hand, stroking my fingers with the tips of hers. Ketty eased herself down into a chair beside the bed, wincing and pressing her lips together.

"Did Davis hurt you bad?" I asked.

"Nothin' time won't heal," she said, never one to cause a fuss.

"You dumb nigra." I scowled at her. "You shouldn't have put yourself in harm's way for me." I had enough guilt to live with. If the men had strapped her to the post, she wouldn't have survived, and I would've added her death to my tally of self-blame.

"Psst." She blew off my remark. "You said de masa sent you and I figured you be telling de truth. And I wasn't about to let dem fools shred your skin lak dey did Primus's."

"And what you be thinking li'l ol' you gonna do to stop two big, strapping men?"

"Stall 'til de masa come," she said matter-of-factly.

I clucked my tongue. "Suppose I love you anyhow, even ef you plumb crazy." Smiling, I kissed Mary Grace's head as she leaned back into my chest. "Is de masa doing all right?"

"Don't you be worrying 'bout him none," Ketty said. "You may have raised him from his bed, but he bin storming 'round dis place lak a madman. De missus running off is messing wid his mind. Et doesn't seem right, you know?"

"What?"

"Missus Olivia running off and leavin' Miss Willow behind. She loves dat chile and dis place. I knowed dat woman all her life, and dis ain't lak her."

Can you ever truly know someone? My thoughts drifted to the missus's secret mission to help slaves. I'd been with her day in and day out, yet I'd been as surprised as the masa to learn of her doings.

"I bin wondering," Ketty said, "why de masa come in his state to rescue you."

"What you gitting at?"

She avoided looking me in the eye and poked at a knot in the cypress plank floor with the tip of her shoe. "Why, is what I've bin wondering." She heaved a sigh like she didn't take any pleasure in what was coming next. "He lets Miller and his men hand out punishments all de time widout much of a fuss. I don't see Primus in here while he mends. You ain't takin' care of de masa in ways men want, are ya?" She craned her neck to study me.

Taken aback by her accusation, I choked back the disappointment settling in my chest. "No. Masa Charles be a lot of things, but he never used me in dat way. I was doing de masa's bidding, was all."

She snorted. "Dere is more to et den dat. I know you, Rita, and dere is somepin' you ain't telling me. What happened out dere when you left wid de masa?"

"Hush, now," I said, glancing around the small one-room hospital as if expecting others to be listening, but the doctor had retired to his cabin hours ago, and I was the only patient.

"See, I tole you. You keeping somepin' from me." She looked at me, imploring me to release the secrets I withheld.

"I...I can't. And I need you to mind your business and keep quiet."

She sent me a long, pained look before looking away. "Have et your way."

I wanted to throw my arms around her neck and

unburden the secrets and lies consuming me. Maybe by confiding in my friend, the torment bedded inside me would subside. But somehow I knew that would never happen. What was eating me up would kill me first, and my punishment, if not at the masa's hand, would come when my earthly days were over.

"Doc says dat I can return to de big house tomorrow," I said, trying to shake off the awkwardness between us.

"Miss Willow be some happy. Sho' glad she got you. I hope Masa Charles be kinder to his kin den ol' Masa Shaw was to Missus Olivia. Even though Masa Shaw loved and spoiled his only chile, he was harsh and didn't care one wit 'bout de tears she shed when he sent me to de quarters. De girl didn't eat for a solid week. Dese masa bring us into deir homes to care for deir chillum, den git right mad when dere kin grow to love us. Sometimes I think dey de stupid ones. Always gwine around claiming we ain't smart, but some of de choices dey make are dumber den what any slave would do. I sho' hope Masa Charles don't do to Miss Willow—"

"What's got dis notion in your head? Have you heard talk of de masa separating us?" Panic rose in me. He wouldn't do that to Miss Willow. With her mama gone, surely he wouldn't take me from her too.

"De day after you got a whipping, he took Winston into town and sold him."

"How you know dat?"

"Masa's driver said so. Heard de masa tell his men down at de wharf to put him on de ship heading to Alabama. We won't be seeing dat man no more. Maybe

da Lard turned his listening ears back on, you suppose?"
She didn't wait for a reply. "And dat ain't all—Sooky was
scrubbing de floors in de library and overheard de masa
in his study talking to a man 'bout selling some of us off."

"Why you only telling me dis now?" I sat straight up.
"Git down, Mary Grace." I patted her leg, and obediently
she hopped off the cot.

"Now, wait a minute. You git back in dat bed." Ketty's
bones creaked as she pulled herself to her feet.

I swung my legs over the side of the bed. "I ain't 'bout
to lie in dis bed while our fate is decided again."

Ketty's brow narrowed. "And what you fixing to do?
You a slave."

"I don't know yet. Maybe talk to de masa."

"You a fool, den. Livin' up in de big house done
messed wid your brain. You ain't got no say, any more
den de rest of us. De masa do what he wants, and ain't no
pickin' ninny gwine to change his mind."

I knew she was right, but I had to try.

I strode to the door. "Come, Mary Grace. We gwine
to see Miss Willow."

Mary Grace grinned and dashed to my side. I cradled
her head to my thigh. Tears caught in my throat as I regarded my friend. "I'm sorry, but I must do what I can for
my gal."

Ketty closed the distance between us; her expression
softened as she took my hand. "At one time...I'd have
done anything to protect what was mine." Tears misted
her eyes. "My chillum are all gone. Either daid or sold off.
Masa Shaw saw to dat. I done things to try and keep us

all together, things I'd do again ef de outcome had bin different." She looked down at my girl and stroked her cheek. "Never forgit how much your ma loves you, you understand?"

Mary Grace bobbed her head.

"Good gal." Her gaze fell on me. "Be careful." She squeezed my hand before releasing it to drop by my side.

I searched her face for the understanding I so desperately needed from her. "You see, Miss Willow, she need me too. And I knows she a white babe, but I love her, deep in here." I placed a palm over my heart, biting down on my lip to cease its trembling. "Lak I do for my gal, I fight for de chile. She got nothin' left in dis world."

"She got her pappy."

"A man dat sails 'round de world and is scarcely home. No, et won't do."

"Et dangerous, de love you hold for dat white baby."

"Dis gal right here," I patted my child's head, "and de li'l miss is de reason I still breathing. Widout dem, death be easier den dis life."

"Mama?" Mary Grace looked up at me, her eyes filled with concern.

"Don't you worry none." Straightening, I smiled down at her, tucking the mess of feelings stirring in me away. "Evvything be jus' fine. Ain't dat right, Ketty?" I cocked my head at her.

"Sho' is. Ain't nothin' to worry 'bout." She smiled wide, revealing big old teeth, but her smile stopped at her mouth.

Entering the back door to the big house, I met

Thaddeus as he was leaving for the night. At the sight of me, his eyes widened like a coon's caught in the glow of a lantern.

"What are you doing here?" he said.

"Come to care for de li'l miss."

"Too stubborn for your own good."

The soft cries of a child came from somewhere in the house. My chest compressed. "Where she at?"

"Masa Charles is trying his best to comfort her but it's of no use, the child's inconsolable. She's been crying for you. With her mama's disappearance, her pa's current state, and you hurt, the poor girl's scared."

"Where's Betsy Sue? She supposed to be—"

"I right here, Miss Rita." The young woman brought to Livingston as a nursing wench walked toward us down the corridor. In the dim light from the lanterns, I noticed her wringing her hands together.

"You couldn't calm de chile?"

"I tried evvything. I don't know what to do. De masa threatened to throw me in de pit for a week ef I didn't git her to stop. But she axin' for you."

"Take Mary Grace. I'll see to de li'l miss." I placed my daughter's hand in hers.

Thaddeus led me down the corridor to the library. He lifted his hand to knock on the partially closed door, but I grabbed his wrist to stop the intrusion. I jerked my head for him to take his leave. He hesitated, then gave a half bow and retreated down the hallway.

Through the opening in the door, I saw Masa Charles sitting in a chair, holding Miss Willow. Her head rested on his chest while her small body quivered with spent sobs. He hummed a tune her mama used to sing to her each night before bed, his voice deep and soothing. His fingers stroked her dark curls. For a few brief seconds I stood observing the man I'd feared from the day he purchased me. It was on the rare occasions when he left his suit of masa and dictator behind—becoming merely a husband and a father and revealing tender sentiments—that he appeared the most human.

I knocked on the door, and the masa's singing stopped. "Yes?"

Opening the door the rest of the way, I stepped into the room. "Masa, Ketty tole me de li'l miss was upset."

At the sound of my voice, Miss Willow's head popped up, and a smile broke across her face. Then she was wiggling to escape her pappy's arms. "Mammy!" Her bare feet hit the floor, and she ran to me. Her arms scooped me around the knees; burying her face in the fabric of my shift, she kissed me repeatedly. "Don't leave, Mammy. Please don't leave." Then the tears came again.

I untangled myself from her arms and dropped to my knees in front of her. "Hush, now, angel gal. Mammy here now. And I'm gwine to take good care of you."

She leaped into my arms, sending me backward to land on my backside, and I winced from the pain of the lashes. I sat on the floor with the child in my arms. She rested her head on my shoulder, and I rocked her the way she liked, ever since she'd been a babe. Her sobs turned to hiccups as she calmed.

I looked across the room at the masa as he let out

a deep sigh and leaned forward to rest his elbows on his knees. He looked as if he had aged ten years since the missus's murder.

"Ef et is all right wid you, Masa, I'll take Miss Willow upstairs to bed."

"Very well." He rose, and I scrambled to my feet with Miss Willow still fastened to me like a bloodsucker.

Her legs wrapped around my hips, and her nails dug into my neck. "Don't let me go," she whimpered.

"Never," I promised—something I had no right to do. My life, Miss Willow's, and that of my daughter's lay at the mercy of Masa Charles. Not to mention all the folks enslaved to Livingston. With the lady of Livingston dead, no one knew what the masa would do with the estate and all those who resided there.

I left the masa to his suffering and took the children up to the nursery. I sat on the floor with my back resting against the footboard of the bed with the girls sitting on my lap, their heads pressed to my bosom. I smoothed their hair and softly sang the song I whispered in my girl's ear each night.

A snow white stork flew down from the sky,
Rock a bye, my baby bye;
To take a baby gal so fair,
To young missus, waitin' there;
When all was quiet as a mouse,
In ol' masa's big fine house.

Dat little gal was borned rich an free.
She's de sap from out a sugah tree;

But you are jes as sweet to me,
My li'l colored chile.
Jes lay yo head upon my bres'
An' res', an res', an res', an res',
My li'l colored chile.

Miss Willow's lids grew heavy, and her body slumped in my arms. I carried her to the bed and tucked her beneath the soft pink coverlet. Lifting her arm, I placed her favorite doll in her embrace and pulled the quilt up under her chin.

Her lids fluttered open. "Where's Mary Grace?" she asked, her voice laced with sleep.

I smoothed back a tendril of hair sheltering her eyes and adjusted myself on the side of the bed. "She's asleep on her pallet."

"But I need her close." I heard the sobs working in her.

I rose to my feet and hauled the pallet with my sleeping daughter up beside the bed. "Dere, now she right beside you."

Disregarding what she'd seen me do moments before, she peeked over the side of the bed. Satisfied, she lay back against the pillow, curled into a fetal position, and clutched her doll tight to her chest. I remained seated beside her after she'd fallen asleep, thinking about how much Miss Willow and my girl loved each other. Even though God had given them different parents and covered their bodies in skin as dark as brown sugar and as fair as fresh cream, their hearts loved each other. The innocence of their love reminded me that beyond the hate poisoning the world, it held beauty. At times life's hardships removed even the smallest reflection of the good from folks' perception, yet I beheld goodness every day in my gals. Malice had no room to seed in their hearts because they were too young to know what hatred was. Such notions weren't allowed to water and grow—Miss Willow's mama and I had made sure of it.

If the masa did right by my girl and me, I'd honor Missus Olivia and continue to nurture her girl in the beliefs of her mother. She believed folks like me had a purpose beyond the price tag the whites hung around our necks. That we were humans the same as the whites, who considered themselves a higher life form than the men, women, and children that ran their homes and estates.

But Masa Charles didn't see things the way his wife had. I caught how his mouth arranged and puckered tight at how his girl doted on mine. I worried a day would come when he decided to sever their bond, and it grieved me what it'd do to them.

On my return to the main floor, I found the masa in his study. Whiskers shadowed his face; his blond hair lay unkempt and dark circles had formed under his eyes. He lifted his head from the ledgers splayed across his desk before I could knock.

His brow wrinkled. "Is Willow settled?"

"She asleep for now."

His face relaxed. "What is it you want, then?"

"May I come in?"

Gesturing for me to enter, he dropped his gaze and dipped his quill into the ink bottle and began scripting on the ledger in front of him. I entered and closed the door behind me. The movement of his quill stopped, and he looked up at me with his unnervingly hard gaze.

Taking a step back, I bowed my head, my eyes dropping to the gold-printed rug under my feet. My stomach had churned with apprehension since Ketty's mention of slaves being sold off, and asking the masa about his business was only asking for trouble—

"Oh, for heaven's sake, out with it."

The drumming of the masa's fingers hurried me along. "I...I...Dere is talk of slaves being sold off."

"The walls seem to have ears. Is nothing sacred in my own home?" he growled.

My pulse raced. "I'm sorry, Masa. I know people git to talking, and evvything may not be said how et rightfully is, but you see, I come 'bout de li'l miss. Ef you fixing to sell us off...well...de li'l miss, I don't think she can handle dat. She already broken-hearted dat her mama done run off." I didn't tell him how it'd kill Mary Grace and me just the same, because Masa had no time for whining from slaves with big feelings.

"Run off?" His voice rose, then trailed off, as if he didn't know whether he was angry or puzzled by my statement.

"Folkses are saying she run off," I said in a hushed tone, moving closer so our conversation remained between us. "Den wid Miller gone, some of de slaves say maybe dey run off together. Or maybe she took off wid a man from her past." Pain scattered across his face and I licked my dry lips, gulping back a breath. I'd done it now.

"What man?" His voice hitched.

I clamped my lips tight.

"I repeat, what man?" The quill shook in his hand.

It pained me to speak the words, but I couldn't take back what I'd started. "Your brother, Masa," I said softly.

"My brother...run off?" His words were scarcely discernible.

Silence fell like a cloak around us. I held my breath, waiting for him to unleash his rage, but when it didn't come, I lifted my eyes.

He sat looking out the window into the darkness, his mind swallowed up by the night. When he did speak, I was taken aback by his response. "That's what we'll say. She just up and left, leaving no note or reason." Relief accompanied by sorrow echoed in his voice. "May God forgive me." He stared at his hands, clasped white-knuckled on his desk. Shame swept over his face and seemed to seep across the room to sink into every fiber of my being. The continuation of the lies we spun shackled us together, and it was in that moment we made the choice to disgrace the missus's memory and allow people to weave the story of Masa Ben and her love affair. She'd be painted as a woman capable of abandoning her duties—her child and a husband I know she loved.

"Do you understand?" he said.

"Yes, Masa."

"Good." He squared his broad shoulders and resumed his emotionless facade. "Changes will come to Livingston."

My eyes locked on his, and I asked, "What changes, Masa?"

He arched a brow and I cursed myself for my forwardness, but I couldn't look away. I needed to know. A look of wonderment crossed his face and he eyed me with curiosity, as if he'd never saw no slave find their voice before. Ketty would be angry at me for putting myself in danger, but the fear of what lay out *there* if the masa got it in his head to sell Mary Grace and me outweighed his wrath.

"You will see. You're dismissed." He vaguely waved a hand, and I knew I'd get no more out of him.

I curtsied and left him to his business.

∾ CHAPTER ∾
Eight

A s Masa had promised, early the following week, three men with a carriage rode into Livingston. I recognized Masa Charles's men from town, as they'd come by the plantation from time to time to go over shipments with the masa.

In the nursery, I pulled back the curtain and watched as the driver of the carriage jumped down and went to open the door. A man dressed in a fancy navy suit stepped out. He removed his top hat, and I recognized the raven-haired man as Masa's lawyer friend, Sam Bennick. He tucked his hat in the crook of his elbow as he scoured the grounds in one quick sweep of his eyes before disappearing around the side of the house to the work yard.

I let the curtain fall at the clang of the plantation bell, accompanied by pounding on the back door.

Davis's voice rang out. "Everyone outside!"

I heard the panicked voices of the house folk rising. My heart thundered. It was happening. The change the masa had spoken of had come.

"Mammy!" An ashen-faced Miss Willow leaped off the rocking horse she and Mary Grace had been taking turns on. Mary Grace stood unmoving, her eyes shining with terror.

A house girl looked at me on her way down the stairs. "May de Lard help us all."

The urge to grab my girl and run awoke in me. A frantic tug at my skirt made me jump, and I glanced down to see my sweet angel gal, her big green eyes round with fright, looking to me for comfort. "Don't you fret none, angel gal, et be all right," I said for the hundredth time over the last few weeks, since everything went awry. "We got to go. Come, Mary Grace." I held out my hand.

Downstairs, we stepped into the line of wide-eyed house folks moving out the back door. Whispers of "What gwine on?" followed by "I tole you we were being sold" reverberated through the corridor. The young girl responsible for filling lanterns and replacing candles broke into sobs ahead of us.

Mary Grace tugged on my hand. "I'm scared."

Stifling my panic, I peered down at her, forcing a smile. I lacked the words to console my girl.

The children and I stepped out onto the back veranda, and I looked over the yard filled with the concerned faces of those rounded up.

"Come on, move along!" Davis said, shoving us toward the crowd.

"Let's go back." Miss Willow stopped, her hands clawing at my arm.

"I said, move!" Davis's voice boomed. He pushed me roughly from behind, and I staggered forward as the flock of house folks scurried to do his bidding, separating me from Mary Grace and Miss Willow.

"Mama?" Mary Grace cried.

Through a narrow gap in the bodies, I saw the girls clinging to each other, tears dampening their cheeks.

"Mammy, I need you," Miss Willow's wail echoed through the barking of orders, weeping, and scurrying feet.

"Let me through." I shouldered between the advancing bodies. "Move!" Panic tightened my chest as the people kept coming, their numbers swelling further with the addition of the folks from the quarters. *Dey gonna be trampled.* I beat at people's arms and chests trying to get through to the babies.

"Henrietta!" Masa Charles shouted, and I glimpsed him over the heads of the crowd.

I gasped for air, never more happy to see the masa. "I here, Masa." I waved a hand high.

His gaze fell on me. "Clear a path. Let her through."

Folks heeded the masa's order, and I raced toward him. He held Miss Willow in his arms, and when she saw me, she held out her arms for me to take her. Greedily, I enfolded her in an embrace. She tucked her head into the curve of my neck. I looked at the masa to find him peering down at Mary Grace, who stood clutching his trouser leg, her eyes wide with terror.

I sprang toward her, pulling her into the protection of my side. "I'm sorry, Masa. She jus' skeered. Et won't happen again."

He returned his gaze on me. "Get them inside."

"Yes, Masa." Pulling Mary Grace along beside me, I headed for the steps.

"Rita!" I heard Ketty call out.

I turned, searching for her, and spotted her standing a few feet away. Relentless tears poured from our eyes as we exchanged a knowing look. She lifted a frail hand in a half wave. Powerless to change what was happening, I mouthed, *I love you.* She touched a hand to her chest and nodded her understanding. Trembling rocked through me, and my legs felt like bags of grain as I turned and walked up the steps.

Thaddeus stood on the back veranda, watching what was happening in the work yard. "You know 'bout dis?"

He bowed his head. "Masa told me this morning."

"Why aren't you out dere?" My question sounded accusatory even to me.

He took me by the arm and led me inside. "Masa said that all house slaves would be sold. Except for you and me."

"And my gal?"

He winced, avoiding my gaze. "Said he'd keep her for a play toy for Miss Willow."

For half a breath, the ache throbbing in my chest over what was happening outside faltered and I rejoiced in the fact that Mary Grace and I wouldn't be separated.

I released Miss Willow to stand on the floor. "You gals go upstairs and play in de nursery. I be up shortly."

Miss Willow shook her head defiantly, and Mary Grace mimicked her.

"I don't want any sass. Now off wid you both," I said sternly. Clasping hands, the girls climbed the stairs. When they were gone, I turned to Thaddeus. "He selling all of dem?"

"I don't know the details, but all house slaves and most of the folks dating back to Masa Shaws's ownership."

"Where dey gwine?"

"Overheard Masa tell his men that they were to be sold at auction in Nawlins. His words were, 'As far away from Charleston as possible.'"

"Surely he can't sell evvyone. Dere be no one to tend de grounds."

"There's a big auction in town next week. Masa plans to attend it. Can't quite figure out what's gotten into him lately. Must be to do with the missus taking off. She always did have a spell over him. Some are saying she possessed him."

"Don't you be acting lak she some sort of witch or somepin'." I jabbed a finger at him. "And don't go blaming de missus for de demons of de masa."

"All I'm saying is, his love for her consumed him." Thaddeus lifted his hands in truce.

"And dat be his choice. Ain't no fault of de missus." I folded my arms.

The sound of the masa's voice turned our heads away, and Thaddeus went to greet him. I dashed into the library, out of sight. The masa didn't like to catch slaves idling by, and he certainly wouldn't be happy to find them gossiping about his family's business. But it didn't matter much; house folk did it anyway. Gossip between slaves leaked from one plantation to another. Us slaves knew more about our masas and neighboring farms than they cared to admit. Secrets were best left unspoken because, like the masa had said, the walls have ears. A fact the whites quickly forgot, because they viewed us as belongings and had become accustomed to slaves hovering in corners, waiting on their next command. We faded in their minds and into the decor of their world.

"Come, Sam, let's have a drink in my study. The day has left a sour taste in my mouth," Masa said. "Thaddeus, go on down to the kitchen house and prepare our guest and me something to eat."

"Yes, Masa."

I heard the men move down the corridor to the study.

Darting a look over my shoulder as if expecting the vacant house to grow new eyes, I tiptoed down the hallway to listen in on the men.

"Are you certain you want to do this?" Mr. Bennick said. "People will suspect something is amiss, with the sudden changes you're making to Livingston. And Olivia—it doesn't feel right, what you're fixing to do. We've been friends for years, but covering up this crime puts my career in jeopardy. Not to mention—for God's sake, Charles, she was murdered! And the sick bastards are out there, free."

"You think I don't think of that? Day and night, I'm tormented with visions of her struggling to breathe as she claws at the rope around her neck. I hear her screaming for me in the middle of the night, and I sit up drenched in sweat. Only to wander down the hall to the nursery to stand over my sleeping daughter, lest she too disappears. These walls will devour me. Every corner of the place is a reminder of her and of what Willow and I've both lost. A reminder of how I neglected to protect Olivia and how, as each day passes, I fail to find the ones responsible."

"Let the law handle this. Extra eyes out there searching—"

"Searching for what? We have no facts to go on, no evidence to point us in any direction. All we have is the word of runaways. And you know as well as I, that means nothing. The only justice we will find in this is our own, and that justice is a fleeting hope, as we have no faces to put to the crime." Bitterness tolled in his voice. "I know I'm asking a lot from you to join me in this ruse. But I don't know what else to do. I've racked my brain for the names of those who would do this. Was it my neighbors, my friends, or my enemies?"

"Do you have enemies?"

"What man doesn't? That's the part that worries me the most: if they're capable of such a heinous act, what next? If it leaks that Olivia helped runaways, I fear for the safety of Willow and myself not only from the ones responsible, but from planters all around. What keeps vigilantes from attacking Livingston when I'm away? My only hope is to let them believe they got away with it, in hopes they will forget about my family and Livingston. Being branded as a nigger lover is a threat I can't risk. All I own and Willow's inheritance will be lost. Willow and I will spend the rest of our lives with the title hung around our necks." Chair legs screeched on the floor, and someone began pacing the floors. "No. I won't have it. No one can find out Olivia died helping slaves. No one!"

"But Charles, to brand her as a fallen woman capable of forsaking all she loved for this story you'll allow to spread about her and your brother...it doesn't seem

Christian. I've known her all my life. She was my friend. Placing her in such a light—"

"I know you loved her too; that's the reason I've requested your help. The concealment of her death is too grand a scheme for me to hide alone. As for my brother, if you recall, her love for my brother was real, and something you can guarantee people will soak up like bees drawn to pollen. After all, the people of Charleston love gossip about such disgraces. If they're busy chewing on that, they won't have time to question what is going on here."

"But at what cost?" Mr. Bennick said before he sucked in a sharp breath. "You're truly afraid, aren't you?"

"It's the unknown—not being sure who to trust or why someone would do this. Did someone come upon Olivia and the slaves by chance? Or did someone aware of her crimes follow her, seeking to exact their own justice? Playing the devastated husband that thinks his wife deserted him is the only way I know how to protect our daughter."

"Shouldn't Ben have a say in all of this?" Mr. Bennick said.

Masa slammed his glass onto the desk. "Do you not think this burdens me? Once again, I've wronged my brother. Even asking him to come here after the wedge I forced between us...it's—"

"You sent word?"

"Yes, I asked him to come immediately. I have no guarantee he'll come."

"But why tell him at all?"

"I asked myself that very question. I guess I felt it was

the right thing to do. After all he has sacrificed, I owe him the right to say his goodbyes. I can no longer see over the list of wrongs I've made in this life, and redemption may never be mine, but maybe this small deed will bring him peace.

"In what I've set into motion, I not only disgrace my wife's name, but his. I bring scandal and shame upon this household, myself, and my daughter. Willow will grow up believing her mother abandoned her. She'll never know she was the gleam of sunshine in her mother's life. She'll never know about *him*. And one day when she understands it all, she'll hate me. Dreaming of Willow's forgiveness is the wishful thinking of a man damned to choices made in the past, things I can't undo."

The hollowness in his words squeezed my soul. I rested my head against the wall and closed my eyes, pushing down the twinge of sympathy forming in me for the masa. I had no more room in my heart for coloreds, let alone white invaders.

I climbed the back stairs to check on the girls. My thoughts remained on the masa's conversation with the lawyer man. There had been no mention of Miller. The lawyer didn't have any attachment to a colored like he did the missus. He wouldn't let my offense go unpunished. Had the masa failed to tell his friend of my wrongdoing? If he had told him, I'd be roasting for my sins with the local planters hungrily looking on, quenching their thirst for colored blood. Why inform Mr. Bennick of the missus's murder but keep my secret?

✂ CHAPTER ✂
Nine

MASA'S MEN ESCORTED THE CONVOY OF FOLKS DOWN the lane and out the gates of Livingston. Miss Willow and Mary Grace's playful chatter from the porch swing cut through the bleakness of the afternoon. Thaddeus and I stood at the end of the stone path. I shielded my eyes from the glare of the sun and rose on tiptoes, hoping to catch one last look at Ketty. Not finding her dear face amongst them, despair and defeat rooted in me. I dropped my head; tears plopped in the dirt at my feet. I realized the price I'd pay to cover up the masa's and my secrets was becoming too high.

I jumped at the warmth of a hand on my shoulder, and I looked up into Thaddeus's face. He nodded toward the grand oak tree whose limbs extended over the pond. There stood Ketty, watching the folks as they were led away.

Why was she not with them? She'd been rounded up; I'd seen her standing amongst the others. Lifting the sides of my skirt, I started running, shouting over my shoulder to Thaddeus, "Mind de gals."

Winded, I reached her. "Ketty…you ain't bin sold?" Hope swelled within me.

She never looked away from the wagons loaded with people or the train of shackled folks walking behind. Sadness tugged at her face, making her age more prominent, yet with all the anguish of the day, no tears fell.

"Why you still here?" I asked again.

"Masa said I'm to go to California. Says et a free state. His lawyer friend has family dere, and I'm to work for dem as a cook and earn a wage."

I stepped forward and squeezed her arm. "Lard be praised." My delight at her news soon faded when she turned with a callous glint in her eyes.

"Why me?" she said.

"Don't know."

"I've witnessed much in my life and I knowed de masa ain't suffering from a broken heart. And I seed 'nuf grieving to know dat what be chasing de man. I was here when he found out de missus was in love wid his brother. I saw how et affected him. At one time, de three of dem were de best of friends. Back den, de missus loved de masa but not in de way she loved Masa Ben. But time allowed her to love Masa Charles in her own way, and had et not bin for her fust love, she may have loved him de way he wanted. After he found out, he used any excuse to stay away from de big house. Spent most of his time at de docks in town or here wuking us 'til we 'bout dropped from exhaustion. He avoided gwine to de missus's chambers, and et was I who wiped Missus Olivia's tears.

"When he got past his anger, he fought to rebuild his relationship wid his wife. Ef she'd run off, I know de man well 'nuf to know he'd be out dere luking for her 'til he found her. Even ef he couldn't convince her to come back, he'd try. His love for her knows no boundaries. I sho' of dat." She stomped her foot, her mouth pressed tight with determination. "So you gwine to tell my de truth. What you and de masa hiding?"

"Et…et ain't dat easy."

"Ef you got any love in dat guarded heart of yours for dis ol' woman you call friend, please, I beg you, gave me dis peace before I leave dis place. I must know what I already know in my heart."

I hesitated. "S-she…she daid." Tears tattered my voice.

Ketty slumped back, resting her back against the tree for support. Her mouth silently repeated the last word. The tears she'd held back released, and she did nothing to restrain them. "I-I knowed et. Who done et? Was et Miller? Did de masa kill him for et?"

I gently held her forearms. "No, you got et all wrong." On edge, I glanced over my shoulder, but the plantation lay near naked of people. And those that remained had gone back to their tasks. "Masa found de missus wid de girl he brought back here. Someone…hung dem."

Her mouth hung agape. "B-but why?"

"Masa thinks et was 'cause she was involved in helping slaves escape. When he found her, he said, someone had tied a sign 'round her neck and marked in blood was de words 'nigger lover'. But dat ain't all of et. De masa found a family of runaways hiding in de grass. Dey say de missus was helping dem."

"But why keep et a secret?"

"Masa said ef someone brave 'nuf to do dis to his wife, he worried what dey do next. Scared dey come after angel gal."

"So, he doesn't think et's Miller? Den why ain't he here no more?"

I hung my head and picked at the scab left on my finger after cleaning up broken glass when the little miss had dropped her drink at the dinner table. "'Cause he daid, too."

"Whatcha mean, he daid?" She stood erect.

"I kilt him."

Her hand flew to her throat. "You…"

"Et happened in de barn de night Masa and I buried de missus in de woods. He tried to take me, and I panicked and jabbed at him wid de pitchfork. I didn't mean to kill him. I swear I didn't. I couldn't relive what Masa Adams had done to me. I couldn't…" I covered my face with my hands and wept. I'd believed by unburdening myself of my secrets I'd feel better, but instead, admitting to my sins confirmed that it wasn't all a nightmare. "And de masa, he help me cover et up."

She pulled me into an embrace and whispered, "Et ain't your fault. Miller got what he deserved. Your heart ain't a murdering one. You tried to protect yourself, dat is all." She patted my hair like my mama used to, and the pang of longing for my family and Big John became smothering. Ketty had said the masa was sending her to California, and the realization that I'd never see her again weighed on me, and my world became smaller yet again.

❧

Mr. Bennick's driver opened the door to the carriage and stood waiting for his passengers. Masa spoke to Mr. Bennick in hushed tones a few feet away as I gripped Ketty's hands in mine.

"Don't waste no more tears on me, Rita gal. Maybe dis new life let me rest my weary bones a spell." She grinned brightly for my benefit.

"I wish for you a life better den dis one here."

She leaned close and whispered, "Never let her gal forget her. In time, tell her of her mama. Promise?" Pulling back, she regarded me earnestly.

I choked back the tears threatening to spill at the mention of the missus. "I promise."

"We need to get going if we are to reach town before dark," Mr. Bennick said as he and the masa moved closer.

"Be sure to ask around town if anyone has seen that blasted overseer of mine," Masa said. I squeezed Ketty's hand, and we held our breath as the masa went on. "He'll be lucky to have a position still if he is fool enough to show his face around here again. I don't take kindly to being left out in the wind in trying times such as those that have befallen my household."

"I will certainly spread the word. In the meantime, you'd best be looking at hiring someone more reliable."

"You have a valid point. Thank you, my friend." Masa leaned in and half embraced the man, clapping his back with a hand.

I threw my arms around Ketty and held her tight,

not wanting to let go. "I'm gonna miss you. I—" Her fingers gripping my scarred back were but a dull ache compared to the fracturing of my spirit.

I felt the slight trembling of her body. "You bin lak a daughter to me, Rita. You and dose gals brought me so much joy." She kissed my cheek.

Mr. Bennick climbed into the carriage and Ketty climbed in after him. The driver closed the door, climbed onto the seat, and the carriage moved forward. In the small back window, Ketty waved, and I lifted my fingers in return. I crumbled inside as the carriage took with it the last glimpse of my friend and renewed the emptiness that struck after each loss of my loved ones.

The masa turned and went inside. For a moment I stood and looked out over the nearly vacant grounds of Livingston. Masa had said that change would come, and the cleansing of his slaves was to be the beginning.

"Come, chillum," I said, and followed the masa inside. "Masa, can I speak wid you?"

"What is it now, Henrietta?"

"Et about Ketty, sah."

"What about her?" Footsteps behind me silenced us both. Thaddeus's shadow darkened the sun ray arrowing across the floor from the front window. "Good, you're here," Masa said. "I require a haircut."

"Straightaway, sir." Thaddeus rushed away.

Masa Charles turned and walked down the corridor to his study. "Take your toys into de parlor. I be right dere," I instructed the girls, and hurried after him.

He entered the study and I invited myself in. "Sah?"

He halted and turned to face me, his mouth clenched in a way that would have frightened me a month ago, but somehow the situation between the masa and me had changed. We were two foxes caught in the same snare, with no rescue in sight. He knew it as well as I and I pushed forward with the heaps of questions I'd been pondering on since Ketty had told me she was going to a free state.

"Why you do et?"

"Do what?"

"Send Ketty to a free state when de others are gwine all de way to Nawlins."

He circled his desk and dropped into the chair. Leaning back, he steepled his fingers under his chin. Time ticked slowly before he said quietly, "Maybe in freeing her, my wife's memory won't be so tainted. Like you, she was an essential part of my wife's life. I neglected to hear Olivia's plea to have her nursemaid care for Willow. I insisted that my daughter wouldn't attach herself to her mammy the way my wife had. Instead of reinstating the slave's position in the house, I kept her where Olivia's father had put her. It didn't take me long to figure out the kitchen house wouldn't keep my wife from turning to her. And it didn't prevent her or my daughter from developing feelings for you. So, in the end, my refusal to see reason caused undue harm. But maybe by freeing her, I can do this one thing right by my wife."

"S-she free?"

"I gave her freedom papers to Mr. Bennick. He will give them to her when he accompanies her to my ship in the morning. I've arranged passage for her, and a couple from town will accompany her to California. In return for their services, I've waived their fare."

For the first time I could remember, happiness swelled within me. Ketty was free. Missus Olivia's love for her nursemaid and the masa's love for his wife had secured her freedom.

"De missus be mighty proud of what you did."

The yearning in his expression revealed his desire to believe my words. Clearing his throat, he waved a hand in dismissal.

I pivoted, but paused in the doorway without turning and tipped my head. "Dis goodness you shown to Ketty be de reason de missus loved you." My voice cracked, but I rushed on. "I hope your love for li'l miss's mama makes you 'member her wid fondness de rest of your days." Without waiting for a reply, I darted from the room.

Masa's good deed charged me with hope for the days and years to come, and in his action, I caught a glimpse of the man the missus believed in and honored until death stole her last breath.

⌒ CHAPTER ⌒
Ten

AN EERIE SILENCE FELL OVER LIVINGSTON AFTER THE masa cut through the plantation like the plagues of Egypt that the traveling white preacher had bellowed about from his position atop a turned-over crate a few Sundays back.

Masa sold off anyone with any ties to the missus, purging all slaves from the big house except for Thaddeus, my girl, and me. Those who remained were field hands and folks who worked in the quarters, far enough away not to know the family's secrets.

The corridors echoed with the absence of house slaves' chatter, and the big house had become a crypt of sorrow and memories. In the quarters, folks didn't sing our songs of deliverance that fed hope into us all. At night they didn't sit around an open fire daydreaming of better times. Instead, at the end of a day's work, they retired to their cabins. Melancholy seeped across the grounds, infecting everyone.

The day the stranger arrived, Masa was in his study, reading the slave catalog for the upcoming auction. Miss Willow and Mary Grace sat on the floor in the parlor, playing. I stood wrapping up the trinkets the missus had collected over the years, while Thaddeus balanced on a ladder, removing the family portraits bearing her image. In performing such tasks ordered by the masa, we washed her existence from the walls and rooms of the estate she had loved. Guilt grew in me with each piece of her I withdrew from her legacy.

The front double doors were propped open, giving me a view of the front lane bordered by the live oaks. I heard his footsteps on the front veranda before he appeared in the doorway.

"Thaddeus," I hissed. "Somebody here."

He frowned, descended the ladder, and strode to the door.

"Good day. I'm here to see Charles." The man removed his hat, revealing wheat-colored hair.

"Masa Charles isn't taking guests at the moment," Thaddeus said.

"He'll see me." The man pushed his way into the house.

"Sir, you mustn't—" Thaddeus said.

I moved in to block the doorway of the parlor as he came to a standstill, his gaze trailing over every last detail of the walls and corridors as if he'd walked into the past. He sighed heavily before he glanced past me to the girls playing on the floor.

Unsure of his intent, I said, "Mister, lak Thaddeus said, Masa ain't accepting no visitors." My heart skipped a beat as I took a full look at him, and my brow pleated. I wondered if I'd seen the man before. After a moment's hesitation, I was sure I'd never laid eyes on him. Then a jolt of recognition made me stumble backward. He had similar facial features to the masa. My chest knotted as I realized the man who stood before me was none other than Benjamin Hendricks, the missus's first love. The masa had said he sent word for him to come, and there he stood. Not nearly as handsome as the masa, but handsome just the same.

Miss Willow spoke, and I turned my head from him to the girls.

"You be the missus, Mary Grace," Miss Willow said. "I'll be the slave." She held out her pale-faced baby doll and took the colored baby allowed to the slave children.

I swung back to the stranger. He stared at Miss Willow. The color had bled from his face. The child was a miniature walking image of her mama, and the masa himself grimaced at the sight of her. But when I looked upon the little miss, I found comfort in seeing her mama's face and mannerisms. Each night since the missus's death, I prayed that the Lord would make her exactly like her mama, planting a love for my people deep within her soul.

"Sah, can I help you," I said.

He looked at me, and the pain pooling in his eyes cut me clean through. "Yes…I'm Benjamin Hendricks." His voice was not as deep as Masa Charles's, and a gentler demeanor surrounded the man.

I looked to the study across the hall to find the masa standing, his hands hanging limp at his sides. His complexion had turned ashen and his gaze flickered from Miss Willow to the man.

"W-what your business wid de masa?" I said, unsure if the masa wanted to see his brother.

Masa Ben didn't seem to mind a slave asking him to state his business and went on to say, "He requested I come."

"Ef you don't mind, sah, you can wait on de veranda 'til I check wid de masa ef he is up to company. He ain't bin feeling well lately."

"It is all right, Henrietta." Masa exited his study. "Please take the girls outside to play while I talk with my brother. Thaddeus, see to it his horse is fed and watered. Then prepare a light meal, as I'm sure my brother is famished after his long journey."

Thaddeus bowed and left.

Miss Willow and Mary Grace had scrambled to their feet in the presence of the masa. The little miss, wanting desperately to be with her pappy, darted across the foyer to wrap her arms around his legs. He laid a hand on her head, pulling her close, his eyes never leaving his brother. The tension between the men hung in the room.

I collected the girls' toys, sneaking another look at the brothers.

"Hurry it up, Henrietta," Masa said with a sense of gravity.

"Come chillum, let's go." I grabbed my girl's hand and went to pry the little miss from her pappy's side.

"But Papa, can't I stay with you?" She looked up at him, her expression hopeful.

He looked at her and smiled wistfully. "I need a few moments with this gentleman, and later, you and I will take a stroll and feed the swans. What do you say to that?"

Miss Willow's face gleamed with delight, and she nodded her head enthusiastically. "Yes, Papa."

"Good girl." His lifted a hand and thumbed her cheek tenderly. "Now you run along with Mammy and the child."

Miss Willow ran to my side and took my hand, more than eager for the time to pass until she could have Masa all to herself.

We left the big house as ordered and for the next hour or so I played with the girls until the brother exited the house, mounted his horse, and turned toward the lane. Catching sight of us, he halted his mount and took a long gander at Miss Willow before he heeled his horse and charged off down the road.

I glanced toward the big house, where the masa leaned against the doorframe. He stayed there until the dust settled. His shoulders sloped downward as he turned and disappeared back inside. Then, I did not know the depth of the fear and pain that controlled the masa. It was the next day that my heart would pull for the masa in a way it never had.

CHAPTER
Eleven

THE MASA HAD BUSINESS IN TOWN THE NEXT MORNING, and as he adjusted the straps on the saddle, he glanced over his horse at me where I stood at the bottom of the steps.

"Allow no one in while I'm gone."

My brow knitted at his request. A slave never allows a guest in de masa's home without him or the missus home. "Yes, Masa."

"I mean it, Henrietta. No one. No matter who they claim to be."

"I do as you ask. And I be sho' to tell Thaddeus."

"Good. I trust that my daughter and my home will be in good hands 'til my return."

"Lak you never left," I said.

He swung himself up onto his mount and rode out. I shook my head at the masa's bizarre behavior and went inside to collect the bed linens for washing.

Hours later, I stood in the work yard, stirring the linens with a wooden stick in the large iron kettle of steaming river water. The girls raced around the yard with two young children from the plantation nursery, playing a game of Ole Hundred.

"Mind you don't trip and mark yourself up, Miss Willow, or your pappy never forgive me," I called out.

"Yes, Mammy," she replied, succeeded by a current of giggles as a boy with one blue eye and one brown closed in on her. Masa had kept most of the children, 'cause they never paid any mind to grown-up gossip. The younger woman who watched the nursery children he'd sold and replaced with an old woman the missus had made him purchase out of pity. Mr. Carter—the father of the li'l spawn Lucille—had intended to drown her in the river as she'd outlived her usefulness. When word reached the missus through the grapevine of slave gossip, she'd sent Masa on the mission of purchasing her. Like me, he had to have decided it was because of her tender heart that she sweet-talked him into saving the slave. Miller had cursed the masa behind his back, said he was a fool for buying a half-dead slave, but I suppose the masa's money hadn't been wasted after all.

I caught a glimpse of the kitchen house over the children's heads, its door open, and my thoughts turned to Ketty, and I wondered how far she had traveled on her journey to her new life. Lost in my pondering, I hadn't heard him approach until he spoke.

"My brother says you will care for my niece with her mother gone?"

I jumped, spun around, and my mouth dropped. "What you doing here? You can't be here. Masa said to let no one in."

He smiled sadly, his eyes following Miss Willow around the yard. Something about the way he looked at the little miss with longing and hunger caused me unease.

"She is beautiful like her mother." The emotion that fractured his voice gave me pause. "How is she faring without her?"

I don't know why I answered him, but I did. "She taking et hard. Ask for her all de time."

He never let his eyes leave the little miss. It was like he was trying to soak up everything about her. "Does Charles treat her right?"

I tensed at his strange question. "Lak she be de most precious thing in de world." Something was off with the man, and his presence became more unsettling with each passing minute. "Sah, you need to go," I said.

His gaze broke from Miss Willow and landed square on me. I gripped the stick tighter in my hand, ready to beat him with it if he got any funny ideas. "For a slave, you're mighty protective of him and the child." His tone was not as frightening as his brother's. The facial resemblance seemed to end there. Mister Ben had the same sad eyes as the masa's, but they were dark in color and gentle in spirit.

"Her mama was good to me. S-she saved me when I needed saving. I owe her."

"A slave, believing she owes her master." His brow furrowed. "I've never heard one speak with such dedication." His expression softened. "And the child—do you also hold such tenderness for her?"

"De li'l miss be de best parts of her folks. She—"

"Mammy, what's that man doing here again?" Miss Willow came to stand at my side.

I looked down at her to find her peering up at her

uncle with curiosity. "He jus' gwine." I placed a protective hand on her shoulder.

"Hello, you must be Willow." Mister Ben held out his hand, and before I could stop her, the little miss reached for it.

A little gasp came from him, and his jaw trembled. I frowned at the man's strange reaction to Miss Willow, as if he had waited a lifetime to see the child.

"Willow Hendricks. My mama is Olivia, and my papa is named Charles," she said in a sweet voice. "Who are you?"

He laughed lightly. "I'm a friend of your mama and papa's."

"Have you seen my mama?" she asked.

Mister Ben's eyes widened, and he cast a look at me before returning his gaze to the child. I pulled her in to my side as he bent to be eye level with her.

"No, not for a while now, but if I had, she would've told me to tell you she loves and misses you."

"Why has she not come back?" Miss Willow sounded almost cross.

Moisture dampened his eyes, and he shrugged, unsure what to say. He stood upright and squeezed Miss Willow's shoulder, then gave me a nod and turned and walked toward the front yard.

"You stay here," I said to Miss Willow. I gathered the sides of my skirt and chased after him, catching him as he mounted his horse.

"Who are you?" I asked, breathless.

"You know who I am."

"You Masa's brother and I knowed 'bout you and de missus. But what your business wid de babe?" I needed him to tell me the inkling chasing around in my head wasn't so.

"I believe you already know."

"I love dat gal," I said. "And I ain't gwine to let no one hurt her."

"This I see, and I can't thank you enough. She'll need the tenderness of a woman in her life, and I suppose she couldn't do better than the mammy her mother so trustingly enlisted to care for her." He clucked his tongue and nudged his horse to turn before regarding me once more. "You're aren't like any other slave I've met before. There's a spirit in you I'm shocked my brother hasn't snubbed out. Our paths may cross again, but if not, I hope you will continue to care for the child with the devotion you bestowed on her mother."

He twisted in his saddle to face the lane, but again, he paused and swerved back to me. "My brother isn't as heartless as he makes out. The extremes to which he was willing to go to protect Willow and all Olivia loved is the proof I needed. I'm responsible for the demons inside him. His love for Willow will be his guide." As though he forgot who he was speaking to, he tipped his hat. "Good day, Henrietta."

When the masa returned, I never breathed a word of his brother's visit. And, thankfully, neither did Miss Willow, 'cause that was a battle I wouldn't win. There was a question burning in me that needed answering, but the timing wasn't right, and so I kept quiet.

CHAPTER
Twelve

IN THE EARLY EVENING TWO DAYS LATER, I WAS COMING BACK from the river when I spotted the masa and his brother standing outside of the family graveyard with spades in hand. Freshly turned earth revealed the recent burial of what I suspected was the missus's body. Tears marred my view of the men, and I lifted a hand to wipe them away. Years of heartache had divided the men, but their shared love for the missus had allowed them to put their disputes aside to see Missus Olivia had claimed her proper place alongside her folks. I prayed her spirit would be at peace.

From my position, tucked behind a cypress tree, I watched the men. After whispering a few words to Mister Ben, the masa took the shovels and headed in the direction of the big house. When the masa had disappeared, Mister Ben's head bowed. A gut-wrenching wail shook his body.

"My beloved," he said, "I dreamed of seeing you one last time. But I never imagined it would be like this." His sobs lessened as he told the missus his final thoughts. "Was this all for naught? I walked away so you and our daughter could have a chance at a good life. I trusted Charles to protect you, but he failed. He should've known what you were involved in." Bitterness ran through his voice. "If only I'd chosen not to walk away. If only I'd not given in to your pleas for me to finish school. If I had stood against your father and fought for you, maybe things would be different. You'd still be alive. And I wouldn't have a lifetime of regrets." His weeping came again and, feeling like an intruder in his last sacred moments with the missus, I crept away, taking the long way back to the big house.

The discovery of what had divided the brothers left me with a new understanding of the yearning that often overcame the missus and the torment devouring the masa.

Missus Olivia had won the heart of both brothers and given birth to the child of the masa's brother. She'd spent her years torn between her love of the two men. Love had divided the family, and the tragic loss of the missus had caused immense pain; I worried it may be too great to heal.

With the heart of Livingston asleep in the ground, the next heir, Miss Willow, became the small glimmer of promise for the future of the family and those who remained enslaved to the estate. The knowledge of my purpose resonated in me.

I stopped, tilted my face to the heavens, and whispered, "I gonna teach her right from wrong. Your gal was born in my heart. Don't you worry none. You rest easy now. I take care of your gal."

On my walk back to the big house, I continued speaking to the missus as if she were beside me.

Climbing the back steps to the veranda, I found the masa sitting on one of the whitewashed chairs, staring off in the direction of the family plot. "Evenin', Masa."

"Where've you been? I was looking for you."

"I sorry, Masa. What you be needing?"

"Sit a moment; there is something I must tell you."

I obliged, sitting on the edge of the rocker next to him. I waited.

"I went by my lawyer's office today, and we went over Olivia's personal affairs. It seems she requested that Ketty, you, and your daughter be freed upon her death."

Freed? I gulped back the thickening in my throat.

The masa continued. "A woman having a say in such a matter isn't supported, but her father's handling of his daughter's inheritance made this different. He set up a trust that stated regardless of her marriage to me, she would have ownership over three acres of this land, including the big house and her personal servants. Mr. Bennick informed me several months back that she came by his office and drew up the papers ensuring your freedom."

"W-what does dis all mean?"

"You're free to take your child and leave. You're no longer the property of Livingston."

My gal and I were free. Sweet Jesus! Could it be? Even in death, the missus had done right by Mary Grace and me.

Every slave dreamed of freedom, but now that I had it within my grasp I was scared. Downright knee-knocking petrified. Where would I go? I had no money, no skills beyond light cooking, household duties, and child-rearing. As I began to digest the information, my stomach plummeted. What of angel gal? I couldn't leave her. I couldn't break my promise to her mama.

"But de li'l miss. Who care for her ef we go?"

"In time, she will forget."

What the masa suggested slashed through me. I didn't want her to forget me. I didn't want her to forget how much I loved her.

"I suppose I'll purchase a new mammy to care for her…"

"But, you can't." I jumped from the rocker and dropped to my knees, hands clasped under my chin. "Please, Masa, she needs me as much as I need her. I promise you, I take care of her lak her mama would've. I raise her to be a fine Southern belle, one folkses of Charleston admire and respect lak dey do you. De Hendricks family will be strong again," I implored him, allowing our gazes to meet.

"You truly love her, don't you?" A variety of emotions crossed his face.

I swiped at my tears. "Yes, sah. And ef you allow my gal and me to stay on at Livingston under de protection of your household, I serve you as though I were your property."

His mouth quivered and he rose, holding out a hand to me. Clasping my hand in his, he pulled me to my feet. His eyes searched my soul before his jaw fixed. "Very well; you have a bargain. You and what is yours will be under my protection."

After that day, many changes came to Livingston. Some good and some bad. It would only be in years to come that I'd endure the heartache of what my staying on at Livingston would cost my daughter. But at that moment, I chose what was best for both my gals.

Missus Olivia remained in my heart and walked the grounds in the form of her daughter. I visited her graveside in the middle of the night, to pour out my struggles and worries about the stubborn child she'd left in my care. My angel gal.

Review Note

If you have enjoyed my work, please leave a review on Goodreads, or the platform you purchased the books from. Your reviews are crucial in spreading the word about my books, and I am sincerely grateful for this support from readers.

THE FAIR MAGNOLIA

NOVELLA FOUR

ABOUT
the Author

Naomi is a bestselling and award-winning author living in Northern Alberta. She loves to travel and her suitcase is always on standby awaiting her next adventure. Naomi's affinity for the Deep South and its history was cultivated during her childhood living in a Tennessee plantation house with six sisters. Her fascination with history and the resiliency of the human spirit to overcome obstacles are major inspirations for her writing and she is passionately devoted to creativity. In addition to writing fiction, her interests include interior design, cooking new recipes, and hosting dinner parties. Naomi is married to her high school sweetheart and she has two teenage children and a dog named Egypt.

Sign up for my newsletter: authornaomifinley.com/contact

Printed in Great Britain
by Amazon

45414495R00073